THE FINAL
REVELATION:
THE SUN PROJECT

RJ TELES

10 9 8 7 6 5 4 3 2

Library of Congress Cataloging-in-Publication Data

Teles, RJ

THE FINAL REVELATION: The Sun Project

Print ISBN: 978-1-48357-020-4 (alk. Paper)

eBook ISBN: 978-1-48357-021-1

Cover design by RJ Teles

Printed in the United States of America

Although this story is based on actual events, the names have been fictionalized
to protect the identity of the people involved. Any similarities to persons living or
dead are purely coincidental.

This book is dedicated to all those who live a lifetime of silence behind the green door.

FOREWORD

I have known RJ for almost five years and we have worked together on numerous UFO investigations. I am pleased to say that I have not met a person with a more impeccable character. His research has always been diligent and comprehensive. As a researcher myself, I can attest to the difficulty of conducting research in regards to the UFO Phenomenon. Original sources are scarce, and finding witnesses in the government or private sector willing to disclose their actual experience is even more difficult. In this book, RJ has obtained both. His decision to use a narrative format to present this factual information has created an action intensive story that will keep the reader engaged from start to finish. This is not a dry academic dissertation; rather it is a page turner that will finally shed light on the true story of the UFO phenomena as told by those that worked behind the curtains. I cannot underestimate how invaluable this book will be to the UFO community in bringing the truth of what is happening in our skies to light.

Michael Pan

UFO Researcher and Investigator

THE FINAL REVELATION: THE SUN PROJECT

PREFACE

The "story" you are about to read is based on the actual experience of individuals who served for many years with military and intelligence organizations in senior level positions; positions that provided access to one of the most closely-guarded secrets in the history of mankind. This highly classified information was so strictly compartmented it wasn't until the information from each of these sources was combined that the broad scope of this incredible story was revealed.

I should note that I was "cautioned" against revealing too much of this information; most of which has never been declassified. For that reason I decided to present this testimony in story form. I was also asked to change the names of the parties involved and classified project names to protect the identities of the people who have shared their incredible experience and their concerns for national security.

The UFO (Unidentified Flying Object) Phenomenon has been an enigma since Kenneth Arnold first reported sighting unidentified objects flying past Mt. Rainier in 1947. So, are all those people who report unidentified objects in the sky just crazy? Surely, there are those who tend to let their imaginations run wild and the vast majority of sightings are simply misidentifications of common objects and natural events. And, it's true some people just live in a world of fantasy. Nevertheless, I am confused by all the supposedly educated people and especially the members of the media whose comments are thinly veiled ridicule of any person who might entertain the possibility of intelligent extraterrestrial (ET) life, let alone suggest one might have observed something truly unusual in the sky. That type of thinking is anachronistic if not ignorant given the recent NASA estimate of conservatively 14 billion earth-like planets within our Milky Way galaxy alone. It is also out-of-date in that a majority of the general population and people of science now believe in the likelihood of intelligent extraterrestrial life.

Then we hear the same old tired arguments; "Even if extraterrestrial life does exist, how could it possibly find us in the vastness of space and then travel the great distances required?" Well, maybe the ETs would do the same we do - send probes out into space and hope to get lucky. And, as far as the science of space travel is concerned, one must realize that mankind has been flying for just over 100 years and has already visited the moon. We hope to land humans on Mars by 2035! What will mankind be able to accomplish in 200 years?

It does not take a great leap to suppose a more advanced civilization may have discovered the secrets for traversing the vast distances of the Universe. And, it is not unreasonable to think that mankind has a long way to go before we truly comprehend the complex design that defines that Universe. After all, until not long ago it was commonly accepted that all life required photosynthesis, then we discovered life forms that thrive deep in our oceans through chemosynthesis. And, most of our oceans still remain an unexplored mystery. Also, just recently, proof of a ninth planet within our galaxy, called Planet 9, was discovered. So, how is it possible that our science can definitively predict what can or cannot exist in the Universe?

It is a fact that much of our science is based on mathematics and mathematics are based on axioms, assumptions which can't be proven or disproven. Now, even long-held mathematic principles are being called into question; case in point, prime numbers. Prime numbers may not be as random as mathematicians previously believed. It was a given that a prime number will always end in 1, 3, 7 or 9. Mathematicians believed those four ending digits were random and always had an equal chance of being the last digit of a prime number, until recently.

Stanford mathematicians found that the probability of an ending digit is not so random after all. When analyzing the first billion prime numbers, they found the ending digits didn't have an equal chance of repeating themselves in the next prime number as did the other three digits, thus making one digit easier to predict than the others. What other long-held mathematical assumptions may be incorrect? Consider also, that the foundations of our science rely on hypotheses and brute facts. Brute facts are facts that we accept as true, but cannot be explained; like the number of electrons in a hydrogen atom, for example. We know the answer to be one, but we don't know why.

The study of UFOs is also axiomatic based on the information publicly available. We can only infer UFOs existence through circumstantial and anecdotal evidence. Thus, it is apparent there are gaps in our scientific knowledge. So, all we can definitively say is that our perspective of the Universe is based on science and physics as we understand it. We must consider that our basic scientific assumptions could be wrong. And, that physics as we understand it may not apply elsewhere in the Universe. Recently, a respected member of NASA's Jet Propulsion Laboratory (JPL) admitted that every day we learn something about the Universe that does not track with current scientific theory.

To be fair, I am not criticizing the scientific community. I know many distinguished scientists who readily accept the possibility of intelligent extraterrestrial life given our ever evolving knowledge of the cosmos, but like most of us, they still seek that irrefutable proof as they diligently strive to understand the complexity of the Universe. And, as we learn more about our own culture, many legitimate questions arise about previously unknown civilizations that predate recorded history and the cosmic connections to our existence they portend.

The truth is the question of whether intelligent life exists elsewhere in the Universe has been answered. And, more importantly, extraterrestrials have been here and their descendants are still among us. That "irrefutable proof" exists, but is often dismissed as too implausible or fantastic to be true and is thus a classic example of the evidence hiding in plain sight.

At a seminar I was asked if I believed the U.S. government was suppressing information about UFOs and extraterrestrial life. There are many people who believe there is a conspiracy within the U.S. Government and the military to withhold information regarding UFOs from the public. My response; I am confident the government possesses much more information about UFOs and extraterrestrial life than it has revealed. There is a considerable amount of circumstantial evidence that shows both the intelligence community and military have been involved in the investigation of UFOs since the 1940s as well as statements from former military personnel which cannot be ignored. In 1978 the CIA released declassified reports regarding their involvement in UFO investigations during the 1940's and 1950's; involvement, that for many years, the CIA denied ever occurred. I have also seen official reports and spoken with high-ranking military officers that lead me to the above conclusion, but I would not call it a conspiracy.

Consider for a moment that the duty of government intelligence and law enforcement organizations is to safeguard their country and its citizens from harm. Likewise, military personnel have taken an oath to protect their country from all enemies, foreign and domestic. While it is true that some of these people are a bit overzealous in their efforts, for most, the secrecy is a commitment to duty rather than a conspiracy. These people firmly believe they are acting in the best interest of their country by not disclosing UFO secrets.

Why? Doesn't the American public and the world have a right to know that ETs exist? Many people would argue that we do. Others would counter that such knowledge would cause chaos, destroying the religious, social and political fabric of the world. Surely there would be some cultures who would view such a revelation with trepidation and others who would leverage it for personal gain, but in general I consider it an outdated notion as a whole. In the 21st century, the concept of intelligent extraterrestrials and space travel is well engrained in much of society through the fantasy of Hollywood and the reality of multi-national space programs. The Mars exploration project has revealed the existence of flowing water on Mars that could support life. Even the Vatican has acknowledged the possibility of extraterrestrial life. The existence of intelligent extraterrestrial life forms does not erode the viability of a supreme being or the foundations of religion. So, why all the secrecy? Perhaps the truth is more ominous than simply the existence of extraterrestrial life, but rather strikes at the core of our existence.

Let's consider that question of secrecy from another perspective. What if a nation was in possession of alien technology and information so advanced it was incomprehensible based on current scientific knowledge? And, what if that same nation was concerned that such technology in the hands of its enemies was indefensible? I was told the solution would be to deny the existence of any such technology and its creators. If the creator doesn't exist, then the technology doesn't exist and it is less likely that anyone will search for it (or try to steal it as in the case of military secrets). To many who safeguard those secrets, the thinking also is that there is nothing we can do to change the reality, so why concern everyone?

That may help us better understand why secrecy continues to obscure the truth and the obstacles we face in getting information about UFOs and ETs. But maybe we are getting some answers; we just need to read between the lines. Once, when asked if astronauts have observed UFOs in space, NASA's response was; "...the astronauts have not observed anything in space that we would not expect to see in space." On another occasion, I asked a high-ranking military officer why the government doesn't show more interest in UFOs? "How much time would you spend investigating a question to which you already know the answer?" was his response.

I have been a UFO investigator and "student" of the UFO phenomenon for almost 50 years. It appears to me that one of the biggest problems today is the overwhelming information clutter created by the UFO pop culture and the so-called experts and "ufologists" who foster that culture. Not to mention the preponderance of web sites and pseudo-scientific organizations that chronicles the apparently daily UFO and related activity without any real consideration for the truth. This clutter ultimately dilutes the facts with misinformation and leaves the real stewards of the truth reluctant to share their knowledge. It is for that reason I decided to present this story. The facts are here. And, in some cases the facts will contradict widely accepted beliefs regarding some of the most infamous UFO events and popular "experts" to the disdain of the pop-culture.

What you are about to read will challenge your sense of reality and change the way in which you see the world. Everything we have been taught tells us this is not possible. Even true believers will question their convictions and struggle to accept the reality presented here. And, admittedly some of this information raises more questions than it answers. But, as we are learning more about the Universe the real question has become, "Why not?"

The people who shared their experience with me were quite sure no one would believe it. But, after they observed a UFO conference, said to me, "The truth has become indistinguishable from the fantasy. Disinformation is unnecessary. The UFO pop culture has taken care of that. So, we've decided it was time to tell our side of the story." Regardless, after reading this story, believe it or not, you will never view a sunset in the same way.

"It is a wise man who knows he does not have all the answers; it is a fool who believes he does."

-RJT

THE SMOKING GUN

DAY ONE

Just outside Boston, Massachusetts, an Old Man and a Priest sit on a park bench on a sunny, crisp autumn morning under a crystal blue sky. The men are framed by towering trees adorned with the striking colors of their autumn leaves. A stately old church stands majestically in the background with its stone façade and metaphorical spire reaching towards the heavens. The Old man appears troubled. "Where did you hear this, Mr. Mendozza?" the Priest inquires. "From an old friend. Can it be true, Father?" the old man asks. "What does your faith tell you?" the Priest responds somewhat dubiously. "That we are the children of God," is the Old Man's reply, but his tone leaves it unclear if this is an answer or a question. The Priest simply smiles and nods.

*   *   *   *   *   *

Across town, Max Park dressed in blue jeans and a light sweat shirt, scouts out the local tag sales. Max is a seemingly average guy in his late twenties with dark, wavy hair and a square jaw who avoids taking life too seriously and often gets by on his charm and good looks. He is a single man who prefers to keep his social life uncomplicated. As a summa cum laude college grad with advanced degrees, his lifestyle belies his true capabilities, but allows him to keep his life simple. Max works for a financial investment firm helping people manage their savings and prepare for retirement; not very exciting, but the money is good and his job is relatively secure. Today, he is in search of any treasure that he can resell for a profit no matter how small because in reality, it is the adventure of the hunt that he truly enjoys. Max spies a Garage Sale adjacent to an old red barn that looks promising. He jockeys his car in amongst those of the other treasure seekers and parks.

Max winds his way through the tables of knick knacks, old VHS tapes and boxes of vintage tableware that line the driveway, carefully avoiding the elbows of little old ladies scrounging for that exclusive deal. A young woman presiding over the extravaganza catches Max's eye. She smiles at Max. "Good morning. There's more in the barn if-," she begins. Their conversation is interrupted by an elderly shopper holding up a small bowl who asks, "How much?" "Fifty cents," the young woman replies. This shopper is no amateur, "Will you take a quarter?" she counters. "Sure," agrees the young woman. The shopper takes a quarter from her change purse and hands it to the young woman who smiles as she pockets her windfall. The young woman turns her attention back to Max. "As I was saying, there is more in the barn if you are interested in tools and old military stuff," she says. "Sure, I'll take a look," Max replies.

Max and the young woman enter the barn. It is a large, shadowy grand hall, with the only illumination coming from the dusty sunlight streaming through the half broken windows. Fractured hay bales, rusted farm tools, water-stained cardboard boxes and junk are scattered throughout the barn. The young woman leads Max to a corner just inside the door. "We found this old stuff after my grandfather passed away," she explains. "Sorry for your loss," Max offers thoughtfully. The young woman nods and smiles appreciatively. Max sorts through the clutter and finds an old, green wooden footlocker stamped U.S. in black on the top. He kneels next to it and unhooks the latch. "That was my Grandfather's. He was in the Army Air Force during World War II," the young woman comments.

Max lifts open the lid. Inside he finds two, blue leather-bound boxes with lattice gold trim sitting atop a neatly folded uniform. Max opens one of the boxes and finds a Purple Heart military service medal, and in the other, a Bronze Star. He gently unfolds the uniform revealing a shoulder patch from the U.S. Army Air Forces 509th Bombardment Group circa 1947. Tucked under the uniform lays an old newspaper neatly folded in half. Max carefully lifts the brittle, yellowing newspaper out of the footlocker. The newspaper is an original "Roswell Daily Record" dated Tuesday, July 8, 1947 with the headline, "RAAF Captures Flying Saucer On Ranch in Roswell Region." "Trekkies will love this," Max murmurs to himself. "He was stationed at Roswell Army Air Field in New Mexico," the young woman remarks referring to her grandfather. She pauses for a moment and then recalls with a hint of bewilderment, "He never wanted to talk about it much."

Max carefully unfolds the newspaper and finds an old, faded 9x12 manila envelope between the pages. He gently pries apart the brass clasp and opens the envelope. Inside he discovers sheets of used carbon paper and a mostly blank sheet of white paper except for some type of scientific-looking notation scribbled on it. The papers appear almost new as if placed in the envelope long ago and not handled again until this moment. Max studies the carbon paper for a moment and examines the sheet with the scientific notation. He carefully slides the papers back into the envelope and returns his attention to the footlocker. Max finds some old photos and hands them to the young woman. "Your grandfather I guess. Very sharp in his uniform," he comments. She smiles as she gazes at the photos and reminisces. "How much for the footlocker?" Max asks. The young woman hesitates. "I couldn't sell Granpa's uniform or his medals and, I really don't think the rest is worth much," she replies. "I completely understand, but I'll give you 25 bucks for the footlocker and the old papers," Max suggests. "Well, OK, it's a deal," agrees the young woman. Max carefully folds the uniform and places it along with the medals in a clean cardboard box that he finds nearby. He places the envelope back in the footlocker and gently closes the top. Max counts out $25 and hands the money to the young woman. He thanks her again and heads to his car with the footlocker tucked under his arm.

Max jockeys the footlocker through the door of his condominium and shoves the door closed with his foot. The condo is a simple two level studio with white walls and a blue carpet that could use a quick vacuuming. It is apparent by the clutter that Max's housekeeping skills are severely anemic. Beneath the clutter, the living room is furnished with a sofa positioned strategically in front of a big screen TV. A smaller love seat sits perpendicular and adjacent to the sofa separating the living room from a small dining area equipped with a small dinette set. A desk with a laptop computer butts up against the back of the love seat offering a view of the TV. A galley kitchen in the rear overlooks the dining area and living room. Max sets the footlocker askew on a cluttered coffee table that separates the TV and the sofa. He tosses his jacket on the dining room table as he heads to the kitchen. He grabs a soft drink from the fridge and returns to the footlocker.

Max opens the footlocker and carefully removes the newspapers and envelope. He sits on the sofa and examines the old newspaper. It appears authentic. The story about the Roswell incident is brief but compelling.

> "Roswell, NM. July 1947. The intelligence office of the 509th Bombardment Group at Roswell Army Airfield announced at noon today that the field has come into the possession of a flying saucer. According to information released by the department over the authority of Maj. J.A. Marcel, intelligence officer, the disk was recovered on a ranch in the Roswell vicinity."

Max lays the newspaper on the table and picks up the envelope containing the carbon sheets and white paper. He slips the carbon sheets out of the envelope and examines them. The carbon paper appears to have been used to type up some kind of report or story. He holds a page up to the light and studies it. He lays the carbon paper aside and turns his attention to the sheet of paper with the scientific notations. Max has seen this equation before and senses there may be more here than simple profit.

Max's sense of adventure arouses his curiosity. He goes to his computer and performs a search on the Roswell incident. He finds hundreds of sites regarding Roswell. "But, is this stuff real and what is it worth?" he questions as if talking to his computer. "Somebody has got to know something about this stuff," Max thinks to himself. Max clicks on website after website and finds media articles, public records, and statements of witnesses and military personnel who were reportedly involved in the Roswell incident. From that he is able to piece together a summary of the events.

According to the information Max can find, in early July 1947, an unidentified aircraft crashed in the desert just outside of Roswell,

New Mexico, during a period of particularly violent and stormy weather. On the evening of July 3, 1947, Mr. and Mrs. Dan Wilmot reported seeing a bright saucer-shaped object moving rapidly across the sky. Mr. Wilmot estimated that the unidentified flying object was about 20 to 25 feet in diameter. The flying object appeared from out of the southeast and travelled northwest until it disappeared over the northwestern horizon. Mr. Wilmot and his wife decided to report their unusual sighting to the local newspaper, the "Roswell Daily Record".

Shortly thereafter, on or about July 4, 1947, W.W. (Mac) Brazel, the Foreman of the J. B. Foster Ranch rode out on horseback to check on his sheep following a night of intense thunderstorms. Brazel discovered a long, wide furrow in the ground and a large amount of unusual debris scattered across one of the ranch's pastures. Brazel also observed that the sheep would not cross the debris field. Brazel took a few of the pieces and showed them to some friends and neighbors. The debris resembled tin foil and extremely thin, glass-like wires along with I-beam shaped pieces of wood or plastic. But that's where the resemblance ended. Brazel was unable to cut the foil and when it was tightly folded, it unfolded back to flat without leaving any creases. The glass-like wires were unlike anything he had ever seen before and the I-beams had strange markings. Brazel eventually contacted the Chaves County Sheriff George Wilcox at his friend's suggestion.

Wilcox examined the debris and suspected it may be the result of military operations and contacted nearby Roswell Army Air Field. Major Jesse Marcel, the Intelligence Officer for the 509th Bombardment Group, was sent to recover the wreckage, which was initially transported to Roswell Army Air Field. He concluded that he had found something that was not of Earthly origin. In other words, Marcel believed the debris was some kind of extraterrestrial technology. According to Marcel, testing revealed that the strange metallic debris was thin, but so tough that it resisted repeated blows from a sledgehammer and wouldn't burn. The slender I-beams were not much larger than the supports of a kite, but couldn't be broken. On July 8th, the Roswell Daily Record's headline story revealed that the wreckage of a flying saucer had been recovered from a ranch in the area. Major Marcel disclosed later that the wreckage had been flown from New Mexico to other bases in Fort Worth, Texas and Dayton, Ohio.

Colonel William Blanchard, Commander of the 509th Bombardment Group, issued a press release stating that the wreckage of a crashed disk had been recovered on the Foster ranch. However, within hours, a second press release was issued from the office of General Roger Ramey, Commander of the Eighth Air Force at Ft. Worth Army Air Field in Ft. Worth, Texas, contradicting Blanchard's press release. Ramey claimed the officers of the 509th Bombardment Group had apparently incorrectly identified a weather balloon and its radar reflector as a crashed disk.

How is it possible that Marcel, a high-ranking and experienced base intelligence officer, for the only nuclear-armed force in the world, could mistake a weather balloon for a crashed disk Max wonders? Not to mention that Marcel was promoted and retired a Lt. Colonel. Max knows the Air Force doesn't typically give promotions to personnel who make such major mistakes as Marcel allegedly did at Roswell. Was the promotion actually a reward for being a good soldier and following orders by supporting the weather balloon cover story, Max asks himself?

Interestingly, it was later revealed that prior to learning of the recovery of the wreckage, Glenn Dennis, a Mortician who worked for Ballard Funeral Homes, a firm that provided ambulance and mortuary services for Roswell Army Air Field, received several phone calls from an Officer at the base. The officer inquired about the availability of small caskets that could be hermetically sealed and for Dennis' recommendations on the preservation of bodies that had been exposed to the elements for several days. His curiosity aroused, Dennis visited the Base Hospital that evening and discovered a high level of unusual activity. His presence caught the attention of base security and Dennis was forcibly escorted from the building by security police. He was warned not to reveal anything he had seen or heard, and ordered to leave the base immediately.

This behavior only stoked Dennis' curiosity. He arranged to meet a friend; a nurse assigned to the Base Hospital, on the following day in a coffee shop. The nurse revealed she had been in attendance during autopsies performed on what appeared to be *several small non-human bodies*" and sketched some drawings of the aliens on a napkin. Dennis reportedly kept the drawings despite her insistence they be destroyed for both their safety. Dennis also stated he was unable to learn any more about the alien bodies and the nurse was abruptly transferred to a base in England within the next few days.

Max learned that according to all reports, in the days following the incident virtually every witness to the crash wreckage and subsequent recovery efforts was either abruptly transferred or seemed to disappear. At the time, this fueled suspicions that an extraordinary event was the subject of a deliberate government cover-up. It was also subsequently reported that Brazel was so harassed by military and government agents that he confessed regretting ever having reported his find to the Chaves County Sheriff. In his final statement about the incident, Brazel made the curious comment that "little green men aren't really green". Over the years, books, interviews and articles from a number of military personnel who had been involved with the incident, have added to the suspicions of a deliberate cover-up.

In 1979 Jesse Marcel was interviewed regarding his role in the recovery of the wreckage. Marcel stated, "...it would not burn...the stuff weighed nothing, it was so thin, it wasn't any thicker than the tinfoil in a pack of cigarettes but it wouldn't bend or crease. We even tried making a dent in it with a 16 pound sledge hammer. And there was still no dent." Despite official denials from the Air Force, officers who had been stationed at Wright Field in Dayton, Ohio, one of the bases to which the wreckage was eventually taken at the time of the incident, have supported Major Marcel's claims.

Dr. Jesse Marcel, Jr., eleven years old at the time of the incident, has often recounted how he saw and handled the material when his father brought some pieces home. Dr. Marcel has produced detailed drawings of the hieroglyphic like symbols that he saw on the surface of some of the wreckage. Dr. Marcel also testified regularly until his death in 2013 on his belief that an alien craft of some type crashed in the Roswell desert in July of 1947.

Dr. Marcel's background is noteworthy. He served as a medical officer in the United States Navy from 1962 to 1971. Dr. Marcel subsequently joined the Montana National Guard as a medical officer in 1975 and earned his Flight Surgeon Wings at Ft. Rucker, Alabama. He was appointed State Surgeon of the State of Montana and retired from the military a second time in 1996. He returned to the military in September of 2004, served 13 months as a flight surgeon for the

189th helicopter Battalion in Iraq, and flew more than 225 combat hours in a Blackhawk helicopter.

"This is wild stuff if you want to believe it," Max mutters to himself. He works his way through web site after web site studying accounts of the crash at Roswell. Max runs his hands through his hair and sighs a heavy sigh. It seems everyone has a story about Roswell. Back to the keyboard he taps some keys. "All these web sites, but they don't tell me what I want to know," Max thinks. Suddenly, his face brightens as he comes upon something different. He writes down the name, "Samantha Freeman" and an email address. Max clicks on his email app and types a message:

> "Dear Ms. Freeman…I found some unusual material regarding Roswell at a garage sale and was wondering if you could tell me what it is and what it might be worth? I have a newspaper, some used carbon paper sheets, and a page with a scientific notation. Thank you.
>
> Max Park   860-999-7777."

Max clicks on the send button and leans back in his chair with a broad smile. "OK, Sammy-girl. Let's make a deal!" he says out loud.

*   *   *   *   *   *   *

Early that evening, outside the dimly illuminated back entrance of a warehouse somewhere near Boston, all is deathly silent. Stars flicker overhead in a clear, moonless sky. An older man clutching a large manila envelope rushes down an alley that runs between the warehouse and an adjacent building. He makes his way around to the back of the warehouse and searches for a place to hide, but finds only a dumpster. He checks the back door of the warehouse and finding it unlocked slips inside, but in his haste neglects to lock the door. Another larger man, bald and dressed in black, his face obscured by the shadows, follows down the alley. He reaches the back of the warehouse and looks around for the first man. Seeing no one he checks the dumpster and finds nothing. He slowly turns the knob on the door and finding it unlocked, enters slowly, cautiously. Moments pass and then, a pistol shot from inside the warehouse shatters the silence. The shadowy figure exits the warehouse with the envelope in hand and tosses a pistol into the dumpster. He pauses for a moment and hoping to confuse any subsequent investigation that he knows will ensue, opens the door and locks it from the inside. He closes the door and disappears back down the alley and into the darkness.

Not far away a sterile-looking, modern steel and glass building sits adjacent to a gray, stoned-faced old church. Inside the building a lone figure sits at a desk in a dimly illuminated office sorting through some files. The man's emotionless face with its chiseled features appears weathered and hard like the old stone church. He wears a white shirt and a black tie. The office seems strangely cold and stark like the man behind the desk. It is a darkly foreboding place with only the bare necessities. The nameplate on the desk reads only, "Corvus".

There is a knock at the office door. "Yes?" replies the man at the desk. A large man enters and stands before the desk. His face is unseen, but from the back it can be surmised that he is bald and appears formidable. He is apparently the larger man from the warehouse. He drops a wallet and a manila envelope on the desk. "The information as requested," he says in a flat tone without any emotion. "You have done well," Corvus compliments him. "A life was taken to obtain it," the man confesses. Corvus acknowledges him with a nod and examines the wallet; "The price for those who keep the faith, Mr. Gideon," he replies dispassionately. Corvus turns his attention back to his files without further discussion. Mr. Gideon interrupts, "We have intercepted some unusual activity on the internet regarding Roswell." Gideon hands Corvus a copy of Max's email to Samantha. Corvus studies it for a moment. "I need to know more about Mr. Park. And, get me our file on Ms. Freeman," he orders.

* * * * * * *

Max strolls out of his kitchen with a microwave dinner for one and glass of lemonade. He sits at the desk with his computer and carefully sets his dinner and glass down amidst the clutter. A small slip and Max almost dumps the lemonade on the keyboard. He brushes some of the clutter off his desk and repositions the glass in a more stable location. Max opens his email and spies a message from Samantha Freeman. "That was quick," he mumbles. He clicks on the message and reads:

"Hello Max,

Your material sounds interesting, but I can't tell you much about it unless I can see it. Would it be possible to meet at your convenience? Samatha Freeman"

"Yes, it would!" Max murmurs with enthusiasm. He clicks on "Reply" and types:

"Yes, Samantha. Where are you located? I 'm just out-side the city. Is it possible to meet at a restaurant nearby sometime tomorrow afternoon?"

Max clicks on "Send" and rubs his hands together as if anticipating some type of windfall.

Max closes out of the email program and opens a browser. In the search bar he types "UFOs". The computer processes for a moment and the browser returns thousands of topics regarding UFOs. Max rubs his head. He moves the cursor from item to item. The list is long and varied. He sees information on Lights in Sky, Local UFO reports, a number of popular UFO organizations, alien abductions and the notorious Majestic 12 UFO files.

In UFO conspiracy theories, Majestic 12, or MJ-12, was the code name of a so-called secret committee of scientists, military leaders, and government officials, formed in 1947 under an executive order by President Harry S. Truman. The alleged purpose of this group was to facilitate the recovery and investigation of alien spacecraft according to supposedly leaked, classified government documents that were "discovered" in 1984. The FBI examined the documents and determined them to be "completely bogus", and many UFO researchers agree the documents are an elaborate hoax. Nevertheless, the Majestic 12 remain popular among some UFO conspiracy theorists and the concept is a staple in popular UFO culture including television, film and literature.

The alien abduction item also catches Max's eye and he clicks on it. Another, almost endless list pops up. Max begins to work his way slowly through the list, item by item. He studies some sites more than others and prints some of the information for future reference. In the middle of his research Max hears an audible clicking sound that tells him he has received email. He switches over to his email application and sees he has received a reply from Samantha. He clicks on the message:

"Hello Max,

I have your address and I think it best if we meet privately. Would it be possible for me to stop by your condo for a few moments sometime tomorrow? Samantha Freeman."

Max cocks his head and thinks for a moment. How does she know where I live, he wonders? He clicks on "Reply". "I hope she's not some kind of psycho UFO nut," he mumbles and types:

"Sure, how about noon?"

Max sends off the reply. Shortly, there is another audible click and he receives Samantha's answer:

"Hello Max,

I will see you then. Thanks. Samantha Freeman."

Max shakes his head and wonders for a moment into what has he gotten himself?

* * * * * *

DAY TWO

The next day, on an early Sunday morning, police cars block the area just outside the back of the warehouse. The warehouse door is propped open. Police officers in uniform stand guard as detectives enter and exit the warehouse examining the scene. Two detectives question the owner of the warehouse just outside the back door. "You say you found him this morning," one detective asks. "Yeah, yeah. I have no idea who he is, or what he was doing in my warehouse," the owner replies. "How'd he get in?" challenges the second detective. "I dunno. My idiot stock boy must have left the door unlocked last night," is the owner's explanation. "But the door was locked! So, who locked the door?" the first detective counters. "I dunno. I don't know the guy!" the owner exclaims again. The detectives mull over the owner's response. "OK you can go. We'll check back with you later," says the first detective.

The owner leaves as a police officer joins the detectives and reports, "No wallet, no ID and no clue what he was doing here. The gun was in the dumpster." The first detective acknowledges the officer with a nod and then walks down the alley and back looking for clues. "Apparently, he wasn't alone," he thinks out loud. "A disagreement between two crooks?" suggests the second detective. "Something's not right. The other crook locks the door when he's done? Very considerate," the first detective mutters rhetorically. "Where's that gun?" he asks the second detective. "In the car," is the response. "OK, let's check this guy out with the FBI and find any next of kin," instructs the first detective as they walk back to their car.

* * * * * * *

Later that afternoon Max lays out the Roswell material in his living room in anticipation of his visitor. He places the envelope and newspaper on the small coffee table that separates the sofa from the TV. He stands and surveys the landscape for a moment. It becomes apparent to Max that the room needs some work. In an attempt to tidy up, Max stashes some of the clutter under the furniture or in a closet where convenient. He slips a baseball bat behind the front door for protection, just in case. Satisfied with his efforts, Max is checking his hair in the mirror when his cell phone rings. He glances at the caller ID and answers, "Hey Jen…. I miss you too and I do know what you mean…. This won't take long and I think I can make a few dollars this time." He picks up a Beanie Baby with a scowl and drops it back on the desk. Max continues, "I'm guessing geeky with glasses and bad hair. Rather be with you." The doorbell rings interrupting his conversation. "Gotta go. Call you back in a few…me too," and Max slips the phone into his pocket. He double checks the position of the bat and answers the door.

Max opens the door to find Samantha Freeman. She is wearing glasses, but this is obviously not the nerd he expected. She has long dark hair tied up in a pony tail, with bangs and black-rimmed glasses that accent her piercing blue eyes. She appears to be in her late twenties and dressed in a black leather jacket, white t-shirt and blue jeans. "Hello, are you Max Park?" she inquires. Max is enchanted and hesitates awkwardly for moment before replying, "Yes, yes, come in." "Thank you, I'm Samantha Freeman," she says as she enters and offers her hand. Max shakes her hand and unconsciously holds it a little longer than necessary. Samantha smiles politely and slips her hand from his grip. She smells like Vanilla. Max likes Vanilla. "Can I call you Sam?" Max asks. "No," she replies flatly. Her manner is all business. Samantha scrunches her nose in silent disdain as she glances around the messy room. She notices the bat behind the door and peers at Max. "Can't be too careful," Max responds sheepishly. "Yes, I understand. I did a full background check on you," she replies. Max is taken aback at her reply and it shows in his expression. "Nothing personal," she says and adds, "You can't be too careful." Max is still a bit smitten, so he just nods with a goofy grin. "Can I get you anything?" he asks. "Why," she replies. Max is befuddled by the response, but is hoping this may work out well even if Samantha isn't interested in his papers.

"Well, the stuff is over here," Max says as he leads Samantha to the material. She sits on the sofa and examines the newspaper. Samantha lays the newspaper aside and slips the papers out of the envelope. She studies them in silence. "Found it at a garage sale," Max comments to break the silence. Samantha doesn't respond. She examines the carbon paper carefully by holding it up to the light and then studies the scientific equation. Max tries to move the conversation forward, "I like to browse around garage sales, flea markets, and you know, tag sales. Never know what you'll find." "How exciting for you," Samantha counters apparently uninterested. But Max is undeterred.

"So, is this Roswell stuff a full-time thing for you?" he inquires. "It's a hobby. I do IT research and consulting," Samantha says as she holds up the carbon paper once again and studies it. "Have you read any of this?" she asks as she looks over the documents. "Some. Looks like a sci-fi story," Max replies. Samantha does not respond. "Well, I'm a financial planner and it's--," he begins hoping to impress her, but Samantha interrupts him. "Unbelievable!" she exclaims and her expression finally turns to excitement. "Well, I do okay-," Max says as he has obviously misinterpreted her enthusiasm. "The date formats and style are all correct on these carbons," she points out. Max finally catches on and his excitement grows. "Really, what's it worth?" he asks with anticipation. Samantha's expression turns serious again as she stares him down and replies, "Maybe your life if you're not careful."

Okay, that was a little dark, but she is cute and I can deal with it Max thinks as he edges towards the baseball bat. "What are you talking about?" a puzzled Max asks. "If this is authentic, I've heard stories about people who will come looking for it," Samantha warns him. "C'mon, it's a bunch of old papers about some crazy sci-fi story. It never really happened!" he counters. "No, it's a bunch of old papers that may prove something really did happen," Samantha replies firmly.

"I need to make a phone call," Samantha says and she pulls out her cell phone. She retreats to a corner of the room where her conversation is barely audible. She glances back and forth at Max as she speaks and her expression is very serious. "Right now?" she questions the caller excitedly. "OK, OK, I understand," she replies and ends the call.

Samantha rejoins Max, quickly gathers up the papers and places them back in the envelope. "You need to come with me," she instructs Max. Max is reluctant, "What? Listen, I just wanted to know what its worth. I got a date." Again he edges closer to the bat. "OK, OK, let's just say I know someone who'll pay well for this stuff," Samantha entices him. Max is disarmed by the opportunity for profit, or perhaps the adventure, or maybe it is just Samantha. "Well. OK then," he agrees tentatively. Max grabs his jacket from the dining room table and Samantha rushes him out the door with the envelope in hand.

THE CONSPIRACY

Corvus sits at his desk examining the contents of a manila file folder. He sets it aside and picks up another labeled "Freeman, Samantha" and reviews the documents. Mr. Gideon enters wearing his customary black suit with a white shirt and black tie, and black wingtip shoes. He stands silently before the desk. Corvus looks up from his work. "Freeman is old news. Park appears inconsequential, but the material troubles me," Corvus announces. Mr. Gideon lays a sheet of paper on the desk. "E-mails. Apparently, they're meeting today," he reports. Corvus lays down the file and looks over the e-mail. He leans back in his chair and instructs Mr. Gideon to put a GPS trace on Max' cell phone. "Keep track of him. We may need to have a talk with Mr. Park and Ms. Freeman," Corvus calculates ominously.

* * * * * * *

Max and Samantha park in a busy Boston strip mall just outside a Chinese Buffet. Max is confused, "I thought we were going to see someone who'll buy my stuff?" he asks. "Come with me," Samantha instructs him. She grabs the envelope, gets out of the car, and heads into the restaurant leaving Max sitting alone in the front seat of the car. Max is willing to play the game, so he hops out of the car and ambles along behind her.

Inside the restaurant the hostess leads them through a dining area crammed with a maze of tables. They are seated across from each other at a table in a quiet corner of the dining area. "So?" questions Max as he looks around the nearly empty restaurant. "He'll be here," Samantha assures him. A waitress stops at the table. "We'll have the buffet," Samantha tells the waitress. "Hey, I got a date," Max interrupts her. "I'm sure she can wait," counters Samantha who then turns to the waitress and adds, "We'll both have water, thank you." The waitress places two table settings wrapped in napkins on the table. "So, can I count this as our first date," Max teases Samantha. "No," she replies flatly.

Minutes pass as the two sit in awkward silence. Then an older, distinguished-looking man in a rumpled business suit winds his way through the labyrinth of tables to Max and Samantha. Samantha stands, gives him a hug and sits back down along side Max. Max grins at her, but Samantha just ignores him. The man sits across the table from Max and Samantha and says nothing. Samantha hands him the envelope. The man slips the papers out of the envelope and studies the material for a few moments. Max just sits there, chilling in the moment and not sure what to do next. The man looks at each sheet of carbon paper. One in particular catches his eye. He examines it closely, glances at Samantha, and then studies it again. Meanwhile, Max receives a text on his cell phone. As he reads it, Samantha glances over his shoulder to catch a glimpse. What she sees catches her by surprise and her eyebrows arch in reaction, "Nice picture," she teases. "She's just a friend," Max replies. "Your friend is gonna catch a cold," suggests Samantha. Max smiles sheepishly as he types a reply.

The man concludes his examination of the documents and then studies Max for a moment. "Who is this gentleman?" he asks Samantha quietly. "Max Park. He discovered this material at a garage sale and contacted me through email. Max, this is Dr. Shepherd. He's been helping me with my research," Samantha explains. Max recognizes the man's name and is impressed, "Physics professor? From the university?" Max confirms. Shepherd nods. Shepherd offers Max his hand and Max shakes it. "What does Mr. Park know about this?" Shepherd asks Samantha. "Not much it would seem," she says impassively and adds "I had only a moment to glance at it myself and thought it best we bring it to you." Shepherd concurs with a nod. Max feels slighted by Samantha's inference and is quick to interject, "I did my homework!"

Shepherd turns his attention back to the Roswell material and takes a deep breath. "Carbons of base log entries, activity reports, materiel inventories, CIC (Counter Intelligence Corp) reports and - the deposition - from Roswell Army Airfield July 1947. All this was supposedly destroyed. And the code name for the Roswell operation is here. No more than a handful know the code name," he explains. Max's expression turns serious. "How can you be sure it's real? Those equations refer to Quantum mechanics and M-theory. M-theory wasn't proposed until 1955!" Max challenges Shepherd. Samantha's expression shows she is impressed with Max's hidden knowledge. Shepherd ignores the question. "I don't want to keep you Mr. Park. I will pay you $100 for this material," Shepherd counters. Max's curiosity is piqued. "Hold on. I wanna know more about this," Max demands. "What is the deposition?" interjects Samantha. "$200. You'll sleep a lot better at night with the less you know," Shepherd responds raising the stakes. "Tell me more," Max demands again. Samantha adds her encouragement with a nod.

Shepherd studies Max again for a moment, and then glances at Samantha. "I don't think that is wise," he sighs and then concedes, "but maybe it is time. I will try to make the arrangements." "Thank you?" responds a confused Max not sure what is supposed to happen next. Shepherd hands Max the envelope. "Guard those carefully. Trust no one except for Ms. Freeman. And, do not tell anyone of this meeting. Do you understand?" he asks sternly. "Yes," Max replies firmly. "I will be in touch through Ms. Freeman. Take care of yourselves," he adds ominously and then leaves. Max sighs and his brows arch as he turns towards Samantha. "Is this weird, or is it me?" he asks Samantha. She just smirks and agrees with a nod. "Well, I'm sure my date isn't talking to me. How about a late lunch?" he asks Samantha. "OK," she agrees and they head up to the buffet.

* * * * * * *

Across town, all is still inside Max's condo when the doorbell rings. It rings twice more. A moment passes, then there is a clicking sound and the door knob jiggles. The door swings open. Corvus and Mr. Gideon dressed in their uniform of the day, black suits, white shirt with black ties and black wingtip shoes, enter cautiously. Both are wearing black leather gloves. Mr. Gideon does a quick check of the condo and signals all clear to Corvus. Corvus looks around while Mr. Gideon pulls out a thermal imager and scans the room. The footlocker catches Corvus' attention. He carefully opens it, inspects the footlocker and closes it gently. Then, he notices the newspaper on the table. He picks up and considers it for a moment. "Heat signatures, must have just left," reports Mr. Gideon. "Search the condo. Carefully. And, leave no trace of our visit. We must resolve this as quickly as possible," Corvus instructs Mr. Gideon. Mr. Gideon nods dutifully and goes about his work.

Corvus carefully places the newspaper back on the table and strolls around the room. Max's computer catches his eye. Corvus sits at the computer, taps some keys and studies the computer screen. Mr. Gideon rejoins him. "There's nothing of interest here," Mr. Gideon reports. "It would seem that Mr. Park has done some homework. Let's track every call on his cell phone," Corvus orders. Mr. Gideon nods. Corvus taps some keys and rises from the desk. He glances around the room and shakes his head apparently unimpressed with Max's housekeeping skills. "Leave the premises as we found them," he instructs Mr. Gideon and Corvus exits out the door.

*　*　*　*　*　*　*

The Police detective's black sedan is parked in the driveway of a well kept two-story home in a suburban Boston neighborhood. Inside, the two detectives sit with a distraught old woman. She manages to talk in between sobs. "I don't know how this could happen. He said he was only going out for a minute," she says. "Did he say where he was going?" asks one of the detectives. "No. He just said he was bringing some old army stuff to someone," she replies. "What's going to happen to me," she laments as she sobs. "Everything's gonna work out," the other detective says as he takes her hands and tries to comfort her. "Do you have anyone who can stay with you?" the first detective asks. "Yes, I called my daughter. She should be here soon," is the old woman's answer. The second detective's cell phone rings and he steps to a corner of the room to take the call.

"Are you sure you don't know where he was going or who he was going to see?" the first detective asks the old woman again. "No, no, I don't know," the old woman sobs just as her daughter comes through the door and rushes to her mother, interrupting the interview. Sobbing, she hugs her mother with tears in her eyes. "Please find the people who did this," the old woman begs the detective. "We'll do our best," promises the first detective and he hands her his card. "Give me a call if you think of anything else. We'll be in touch regarding the arrangements after the autopsy." He joins the second detective who has just completed his phone call. As the detectives reach the door, the old woman calls out to them, "He did say one thing. He had to get rid of his stuff before they come for him. I don't know what that meant. I don't know who 'they' were," she breaks into tears again and her daughter embraces her.

The two detectives step outside. "Wait till you hear this," says the second detective. They walk down the steps and get into their car. "Whattaya got?" the first detective asks. "FBI says this guy was a vet, Counter Intelligence Corp just after World War II. Apparently he was involved in some secret stuff. They're turning the whole thing over to the Air Force Office of Special Investigations," the second detective reports and adds, "They'll be in touch." "AFOSI! What the hell?" the first detective exclaims. The second detective has no answer and just shakes his head and shrugs. Why, wonders the first detective, is AFOSI interested in this seemingly average man?

It is unusual for the Air Force to be involved in local crime. AFOSI is the United States Air Force Office of Special Investigations. It is described as a U.S. federal law enforcement agency that reports directly to the Office of the Secretary of the Air Force. AFOSI operates on a worldwide basis conducting criminal investigations, intelligence and counterintelligence operations as well as special operations which are typically outside traditional military areas of involvement. What is unknown to most people and even many members of AFOSI, is that a very select group of AFOSI agents are involved in the top secret investigation of unidentified aircraft with extraterrestrial as well as terrestrial origins in support of NASIC (National Air and Space Intelligence Center). AFOSI is also involved in maintaining the security of all information regarding such operations.

AFOSI's resources are virtually unlimited. The Defense Cyber Crime Center (DC3) was established as an entity within the Air Force Office of Special Investigations in 1998. DC3 provides digital and multimedia forensics, cyber investigative training, research, development, test and evaluation, and cyber analytics for the Department of Defense (DoD). These missions include information assurance and critical infrastructure protection, law enforcement and counterintelligence, document and media exploitation, and counterterrorism. In addition, DC3 is a national cyber center and serves as the operational focal point for the Defense Industrial Base Cyber Security and Information Assurance Program (DIB CS/IA Program). DC3 as well as the resources of the FBI, NSA, CIA, NASIC and even NASA are available to AFOSI agents to support their ET mission.

*   *   *   *   *   *   *

Back at the Chinese buffet, Max and Samantha eat in silence. Samantha's cell phone chirps like a Star Trek communicator breaking the silence and indicating she has a call. She answers and turns quickly away from Max so he cannot overhear her conversation. "When? OK, I understand," she replies. Samantha puts away her phone and smiles contritely at Max. "Work, I have to go," she says. She gets up, pulls a ten dollar bill from her pocket and drops it on the table. "Wait, we were just-," Max moans. "Sorry. I'll be in touch," Samantha apologizes. "At least let me pay for lunch," Max offers. "No, then you'll want to call it a date," she says as she grins and hurries away. "Wait, I don't have a ride!" Max complains. Samantha disappears out the door. "Might as well get my money's worth," Max mutters to himself. He stuffs the ten dollar bill in his pocket and heads back to the buffet.

* * * * * * *

Samantha parks in a lot adjacent to an ordinary-looking corporate office building by all appearances. She gets out of her car and hurries inside. Samantha enters the building, pulls an ID card from her jacket pocket, and clips it to her jacket as she approaches the guard's station. The guard checks the ID. "All set Captain," he says and buzzes her in. She nods and disappears behind some formidable looking polished steel double-doors. Samantha enters the offices of Giga Technology Consulting (GTC) and strides down a hallway lined with cubicles occupied by seemingly ordinary people working at their desks.

Samantha enters a windowless conference room with a long, polished wooden conference table where two men are waiting for her. One is dressed in a suit and he holds a manila file and some papers. His name is Carbonetti and he works for the FBI. The other is an Air Force Colonel dressed in uniform. She closes the door behind her. "Thank you for coming so quickly, Capt. Greene," Carbonetti greets her. Samantha nods politely, but it is apparent that she is uncomfortable with the man. "Good to see you, Sam," the Colonel adds. "Nice to see you again sir," she replies and shakes the Colonel's hand.

Samantha was only thirteen when the 9/11 tragedy occurred in New York, but right then she decided she wanted to serve her country. She joined the Air Force directly out of college with a master's degree in software engineering. Samantha was immediately put to work providing cyber systems security. She was good at what she did and advancement came quickly. When a job in Special Investigations was offered to her she did not hesitate. It was a promotion and a genuine opportunity to protect her country. Until now, her assignments have been simple cases involving breeches of security and theft of materiel.

Carbonetti takes a seat and slides the file across the table towards Samantha. Samantha and the Colonel join Carbonetti at the table and she opens the file. "William Carlson, Counter Intelligence. 1945 to 1955," Carbonetti narrates and then adds, "He was stationed at-." "Wait. Let me guess. Roswell Army Airfield," Samantha interjects. "Right. And he was apparently involved in the whole operation," the Colonel adds. "Thunderhead?" Samantha inquires. The Colonel nods affirmatively, but appears surprised Samantha knows that name. "He was found dead yesterday under suspicious circumstances," Carbonetti reports. "The Police contacted the FBI and they passed it on to us," the Colonel explains. "Are they aware of his connection?" Samantha asks. "No. His file was sealed because of his Intel connections. SOP," Carbonetti answers.

Carbonetti slides the papers across the table to Samantha, "The preliminary police report. His wallet and ID were missing, no other evidence, no witness, and no suspects," he reports. She examines the file and the police report. "Corvus?" Samantha inquires. "We don't know yet, but we have to find out. The Roswell connection may be a coincidence," the Colonel replies. Samantha looks at him with arched brows silently questioning that logic. She has seen Corvus' work before and has little doubt he is involved.

"We have to be very careful. Remember Corvus is connected to some of the world's largest religious groups and he'll stop at nothing to get what he wants. He's extremely dangerous, Samantha," the Colonel cautions. Samantha nods and then reveals, "I just met a guy who found some Roswell documents. It appears to be pretty hot." "Is that where you learned the code name," the Colonel inquires. Samantha nods again. "Can you get a hold of it?" the Colonel asks. "Not without raising suspicion," she replies and adds, "We're working with Shepherd. I think he's about to give us the whole story." "OK, stay with it," the Colonel orders. "Keep an eye on that guy. If he has what you think, Corvus will come looking for him," Carbonetti warns her. Samantha nods. "I gotta go!" she insists and abruptly rushes out of the room.

Samantha has never met Corvus, but knows he is ruthless at guarding some mysterious secret. He always seems to appear when new information regarding the existence of extraterrestrial life is found. Exactly who he is, is unclear. The limited background information Samantha has been able to dig up on Corvus has obviously been fabricated. Samantha's assignment has been to find answers to both Corvus' mission and the secret he so ruthlessly protects.

Outside the building, Samantha takes off her ID badge and stuffs it in her pocket. She pulls out her cell phone as she walks to her car and taps in Max's number. Max is just stepping out of a taxi at his condo when his phone rings. He hands the driver a bill and answers the phone as he walks up the steps to his condo. "Hi Max. It's Samantha. Sorry I had to leave so abruptly. It was rude," she apologizes. "I had to take a taxi to get home," replies an agitated Max. "Let me make it up to you. Maybe if you're not doing anything how about getting back together for dinner," is Samantha's offer. "Hey, I'm on vacation for the next two weeks so I'm free," Max replies. "OK, I'm just talking about dinner now," Samantha clarifies playfully. "Can we call it a date," Max taunts her. Samantha ignores the question, "Let's keep it simple. How about pizza at your place?" she suggests.

"Works for me," says Max. "I'll get the pizza and see you around six," she adds. Max hangs up with a broad smile. Samantha hangs up and stares at the phone for a moment. She has become deeply concerned for Max's safety. Blissfully unaware of the situation, Max unlocks the door to his condo and heads straight to the kitchen. He slips a bottle of wine into the fridge to chill and grins.

* * * * * * *

Back in the conference room Carbonetti paces while the Colonel sits at the table and casually thumbs through the file. "I don't get it. Corvus always seems to be a step ahead of us," the Colonel laments. "Why don't we just pick him up and have a little talk with him," Carbonetti suggests. "On what grounds?" the Colonel challenges him. "How do we explain that we believe the church is involved in some bizarre cover-up of extraterrestrial life and we think this man is their enforcer? Only a handful of people know about our project," the Colonel replies, and then adds, "Besides they're hiding something bigger than just the existence of ETs." "At this rate you'll never know," Carbonetti argues. "This has been going on for a thousand years. We'll get it," the Colonel responds confidently. "In the meantime, we have our own secrets to worry about," he remarks.

The secret the Colonel refers to is the reality that Roswell was not the U.S. military's first or last exposure to UFOs. Unidentified objects were observed over Los Alamos throughout the Manhattan Project causing great concern. However, it was determined after a frantic investigation by the military and the CIC that the flight characteristics of these objects were beyond even the capabilities of the Nazis and therefore did not pose a security risk. This was perhaps more of a rationalization in as much as it was also determined there was little that could be done about the objects. The reappearance in Roswell, while not expected, was also not a surprise.

Unfortunately, over the years much of the Roswell information was misplaced or buried deep in secret files with code names known only to an elite few, and then forgotten in typical government fashion. The "mainstream" military lost track of the files when the few people who possessed the knowledge took the secrets to their graves. Over time, witnesses who have tried to share their knowledge about Roswell have been unable to substantiate their stories without the code names necessary to locate the classified files containing the corroborating evidence. And, others are too afraid to reveal the secrets for fear of being arrested or losing their GI benefits and pensions. Nevertheless, the mainstream military became concerned with the growing number of people coming forward because they were unable to assess their claims without the information from the official files.

Then there was the question of UFO reports in general. Project Blue Book provided no insight because it was primarily a superficial attempt to allay public concern over the UFO issue. The real investigations were never publicly disclosed and most of the military had no access to the information, or were aware it existed. The truth is that although Blue Book was discontinued, military commanders believed there were enough unidentified events to warrant some type of response or ongoing assessment of the situation. These concerns were passed on to higher levels of the military where it was decided an ultra secret, special investigations operation would be created to reconstruct the historical information as well as collect and secure new intelligence. All UFO-related concerns and questions would be handled exclusively by this group and even their existence was to be classified top secret. Any UFO reports are submitted through the usual military intelligence channels and then passed on to this group. The group's reports are classified top secret at the highest levels and their access is severely restricted to only military and intelligence personnel. The initial problem was reassembling the old information and monitoring new events on a covert basis, as well as managing the security of classified ET secrets. And, it was essential that all data be highly compartmented so that no agent would have knowledge of the whole ET story; only their area of responsibility. Even Samantha is not aware of all the facts behind Roswell. Also, as part of this ongoing operation, it was directed that investigators would pose as journalists, engineers, doctors and any other occupations deemed necessary to gather data from both the public and private sectors.

To accomplish this mission, some of these classified operations include creating private corporations as a front for intelligence gathering, and establishing a shield for that activity against the authority of the Freedom of Information Act (FOI). The FOI can be applied only against government entities and thus private corporations are immune. These activities are called "carve-out" projects, also known as Government Intelligence Gathering and Assessment operations to those in the intelligence community. To the public they look like ordinary companies providing everyday business services. Some well-known figures within the UFO pop-culture and UFO organizations work covertly for these corporations even as their alter ego publicly stokes the UFO culture. GTC, the company that employs Samantha, is one such corporation whose cover is that of an information technology research and consulting firm. Not all the employees at GTC are government operatives; some actually perform IT work to maintain the façade. Interestingly, any revenues from these corporations are used to fund the black budget.

Any information and activity regarding UFOs and ETs are classified Top Secret. There are seven basic security classifications to protect sensitive information and operations. These include: Top secret (TS), Secret, Confidential, Restricted, Official, Clearance, and Compartmented information. Top secret is the highest classification level for information and can be further compartmented requiring a specific clearance level after top secret for access. Top Secret material is defined to cause "exceptionally grave damage" to national security if made public. Security classifications should not be confused with clearance levels such as SCI (Sensitive Compartmented Information) or SAP (Special Access Programs). A Top Secret project may be categorized as TS/SCI meaning it is Top Secret and requires SCI clearance. TS/SCI would be the highest security clearance level. SCI can be further divided into control systems, which can be subdivided into compartments and sub-compartments usually identified by a classified codeword. For example, SI (Special Intelligence) is a control system addressing communications intelligence, which has several compartments including VRK (Very Restricted Knowledge), which in turn may be identified by specific code words. In UFO folklore, UMBRA is alleged to be a classification related to government UFO activity, when in reality it was a code word for identifying the most sensitive communications intelligence having to do with conventional communications intercepts.

* * * * * * *

Later that night Samantha parks outside Max's condo on a moonlit evening. She gets out of her car and places her foot on the door jam. She is dressed up in navy blue slacks, a silk blouse and a blazer. She slides up her pant leg and removes a small pistol from an ankle holster. She ejects the ammunition clip, checks it and replaces it with a click. Samantha slips the pistol back in the holster and adjusts her pants leg. She tucks a purse under her arm, grabs the pizza and a bottle of soda, and kicks the car door shut.

Inside the condo it is apparent that Max has cleaned the place. The carpet has been vacuumed, the clutter is gone and the coffee table has been polished. The footlocker is tucked neatly alongside the sofa. The TV is on and tuned to a football game. Max is dressed neatly in a button down shirt and khakis, and it is obvious he is dressed to impress Samantha. With his hands on his hips, he gives the room a once over glance and is satisfied with his efforts. The door bell rings. Max checks his hair in the mirror quickly, and then opens the door to find Samantha holding the pizza and bottle of soda. She looks great is all he can think. She smiles and somehow it seems warmer this time. There is an attraction here that Max cannot deny, but he tempers his enthusiasm remembering how he crashed and burned on the first encounter.

"Come on in," Max says as he takes the pizza from Samantha. He places the pizza on the dining room table and heads into the kitchen. Samantha slips off her blazer and lays it on a chair. She smiles and nods her approval as she looks around the freshly cleaned room. "We can eat at the table or on the sofa. I'm sure I can find a movie or something," Max suggests. "I'm good with the football," Samantha replies as she sets the bottle on the table. "You like football?" reaffirms a surprised Max. "Yeah, I like football," Samantha reassures him.

Max rummages through the kitchen to find some paper plates and cups which he places on the dining room table alongside the pizza. He pops open the pizza box, grabs a paper plate, and then tugs at a piece of pizza while Samantha pours the soda. Samantha steps in to assist him by using a plastic knife to neatly separate the pieces. They sit on the sofa eating their pizza and Max gazes at Samantha. She catches Max's stare and cocks her head silently inquiring as to what is on his mind? "A few hours ago I wasn't even on your top ten least likable list. So, what changed?" Max asks. "You," Samantha replies firmly. Max is not sure what Samantha means. He shakes his head in confusion with an expression that encourages an explanation. "You didn't take the money from Shepherd. Most guys I know would've taken the money and run," Samantha confesses. "Maybe I thought I could get more," Max argues. "No, you would've asked," she counters and adds, "You were curious even though Shepherd warned you it could be dangerous. I just thought I'd like to know that guy a little better." "It's that simple?" Max asks. "Not quite, but I thought maybe we could start over," Samantha replies with a smile. "Okay. Hi, I'm Max Park," Max says holding out his hand. "Hello, I'm Samantha Freeman. Nice to meet you," Samantha responds politely as she shakes his hand. "Can I call you Sam?" Max tries again. Samantha cocks her head and smirks. "Sure," she replies. An awkward moment passes and they turn their attention back to the game on TV. "What about your girlfriend?" Samantha inquires coyly. "She's not talking to me, but it wasn't a serious relationship," Max confesses. Samantha nods and grins followed by more awkward silence as they watch the game.

"So, what do you think about all these UFO stories?" Max asks. "I've been fascinated by the UFO stuff since I was a kid. Ever since I was a little girl, I look up at the stars and wonder if there are people out there? I wonder what their world is like. Do they have families? Do they know we're here? Wouldn't you like to know? Some of the UFO stories are nonsense, but I think there are some real mysteries to be solved. Keeps me busy when I'm not working," Samantha explains. "Who do you work for?" Max asks. Samantha hesitates for a moment. "I do research and consulting on IT problems. You know, I got into computers because of Star Trek," she replies coyly, changing the subject. "What about you? How does a guy with graduate degrees in mathematics and engineering end up working as a financial consultant?" Samantha asks provocatively. Max smiles contritely.

Apparently Samantha has done her homework. Not many people are aware of Max's background. With cum laude graduate degrees in mathematics and engineering he is not the typical financial consultant, but he makes a good living and his life remains uncomplicated. There is more to Max than meets the eye and perhaps it is Samantha's own secret life that spurs her curiosity. "I wasn't really interested in working for an insurance company building actuarial models, or designing the refrigerator of the future," is Max's explanation. "There are other areas of research," Samantha counters. "Sure, at universities where I have to play political games and write esoteric papers that contribute to the school's bottom-line while I struggle to make a living," Max protests.

Samantha gazes into Max's eyes and cocks her head looking for more. "OK, to be honest, when I was a kid I wanted to be an astronaut, but as I got older that didn't seem realistic. I have to admit the Universe is far too big for us to be the only ones, but I guess I got caught up in the day to day and lost that sense of wonder. Now it all seems a little crazy. But if you think Shepherd really has the answers, I'm willing to listen," Max confesses. "I'm not sure, but it might change your view of the world," Samantha suggests playfully. "Look, I'm not the kind of guy who is gonna save the world," he concedes with a smile. Samantha looks at him with a woman's intuition, smiles and says, "I'm not so sure." Max is somewhat confused, but appreciates the compliment which leads him to believe the night is looking good! "For the record, I'm more of a Star Trek guy, too," Max reveals. Samantha smiles at him. The Bears and Packers are playing and Max turns his attention to the TV. "Who do you like?" he asks Samantha. "Packers, no question," she shoots back confidently. Max grins at her. Apparently, this girl really does know football Max thinks to himself!

Max sneaks sideways glances at Samantha as they watch the game. She senses his gaze and there is an awkward moment when she turns and catches him mid-glance. Face to face, her quizzical expression forces Max to break the silence. He covers his real fascination for her by asking, "So, what do you think about all this drama over my stuff?" Samantha pauses for a moment and gathers her thoughts. "I think there is a more to this than we know and it's been going on for centuries," is her answer. "Shepherd may be able to tell us a lot more if you're willing to take the risk," she adds. "What risk? You keep saying that," Max inquires.

Samantha pauses again and then stares deep into his eyes. "There are secrets and people who want those secrets to stay secrets. It seems they will do anything to make that happen," is her answer and a warning. Max can see the seriousness in Samantha's eyes. "OK, let's say I believe you," he responds. "I still want to know more and I'd like to have you make that trip with me. You know, you can keep an eye on me so I don't do anything stupid or offend people," he says. She smiles at him, squeezes his hand and agrees, "I do know." She looks at Max and realizes this just became more than a job.

"Before we meet with Shepherd again, can you give me a little background on what I should know?" Max asks. "Sure," Samantha replies. Max stares at her waiting for more information. "Now?"

Samantha exclaims. "Why not?" is Max's reply. He quickly retrieves a pile of papers from the computer table that contain the information he has printed from his internet research, and hands them to Samantha. Samantha looks over his efforts. "You might want to get another piece of pizza. This is going to take a while," she teases.

Max gets his pizza and settles in next to Samantha. She begins by explaining that the modern era of UFOs began in 1947 when Kenneth Arnold first saw silvery objects skip across Mt. Rainier in Washington State, but in reality the mystery goes back thousands of years based on historical documents and von Däniken's ancient astronaut theory. In his 1968 book, *Chariots of the Gods?*, von Däniken suggests that extraterrestrials or "ancient astronauts" visited Earth and influenced early human culture. Von Däniken also speculates that megalithic structures such as the Egyptian pyramids, the city of Tiwanaku in Bolivia and artifacts from that period represent a higher technological knowledge than is presumed to have been possessed by the ancient people who allegedly designed and built those megaliths. Samantha adds that von Däniken also points to ancient artwork throughout the world that seemingly depicts astronauts, aircraft and space vehicles as well as extraterrestrials and complex technology. Based on re-interpretations of the Bible's Old Testament and other ancient texts, he also believes the origins of religions can be traced to contact with an alien race.

"One problem has been, it can't be, therefore it isn't," is Samantha's contention. Max is confused. She explains that in his 1977 book, *The UFO Report*, Dr. J. Allen Hynek wrote, "Governments from around the world have taken the position of 'it can't be, therefore, it isn't' and have sought to protect and insulate themselves from criticism...' regarding the UFO phenomenon. "Unfortunately, many in the scientific and journalistic communities followed that approach and still do when considering a UFO report or the possible existence of intelligent extraterrestrial (ET) life," is Samantha's assertion. Dr. Hynek was a professor of astronomy at Northwestern University and was the lead scientific advisor for the U.S. Air Force Project Blue Book. Dr. Hynek became one of the world's leading authorities and researchers on the UFO phenomenon. Interestingly, he began by debunking UFO reports for the U.S. Government, but soon realized that some of the reports were, in reality, unexplainable. As a result of his experiences, Hynek founded the Center for UFO Studies in 1973.

Dr. Josef Allen Hynek was born on May 1, 1910 and died in April of 1986. He was an astronomer, professor, and perhaps best remembered as a central figure in UFO research. Hynek served as scientific adviser for three consecutive UFO projects conducted by the U.S. Air Force, which included: Project Sign (1947 to 1949), Project Grudge (1949 to 1952), and Project Blue Book (1952 to 1969). Subsequently, he conducted independent UFO research and developed the original three-stage "Close Encounter" classification system. When the Air Force hired Hynek for Project Sign, he admitted he was skeptical of UFO reports. He suspected that they were submitted by unreliable witnesses, or by persons who had misidentified man-made or natural objects. In 1948, Hynek was quoted as saying that "the whole subject seems utterly ridiculous," and predicted it was a fad that would soon pass. Hynek's opinions about UFOs slowly but gradually shifted after examining hundreds of UFO reports over the decades, including some made by credible witnesses such as astronomers, pilots, police officers, and military personnel. This lead Hynek to conclude that some reports represented genuine evidence.

According to Samantha, the UFO phenomenon, in general can be categorized into six specific areas of interest: Unidentified Objects in the Sky and Underwater; UFO Crash and Retrievals; UFOs and Governments; Close Encounters and Abductions; Ancient Astronauts; and, UFOs and the Pop Culture.

"So, the question becomes, how do we approach the study of the UFO Phenomenon and ET life?" Samantha asks Max. Max has no answer and simply shakes his head and shrugs. Samantha suggests some options. Metaphysics? Crypto-science? Crypto-cosmology or crypto-astronomy? She reasons that meta-physics may help us to better understand what questions to ask or the implications of those questions, but does not promise answers. Any form of crypto-science might be appropriate, but too often our limited understanding of universal physics clouds our vision. She argues that it is widely acknowledged some of our commonly accepted scientific principles are based on brute facts, facts we can't explain but are true, and we have no way of knowing if such facts are consistent throughout the Universe. Nevertheless, we tend to try to adapt or interpret new discoveries in ways that conform to our science instead of considering a new paradigm. "In other words, we use our current knowledge as the basis for explaining new discoveries when that basis may be incorrect" is Samantha's observation. "This is similar to ancient civilizations ascribing ET technology to the work of the Gods because they had no knowledge of advanced science," she contends.

The lecture continues as Samantha submits that perspective is relative to the point from which one starts. Her point is that our own ancient history is now being (re)interpreted based on our current level of scientific knowledge and technology versus 19th or early 20th century thinking. According to Sir Arthur Clarke, "Any sufficiently advanced technology is indistinguishable from magic" and thus earlier cultures may have viewed the advanced technology of extraterrestrials as magic and recorded it as such. Samantha's concern is that we may have been misinterpreting obvious evidence regarding extraterrestrial life and its impact on Earth for decades. At the same time, Samantha points out that another problem today is in fact the advancement of technology. In regards to alleged UFO incidents, it has become difficult to determine whether we are witnessing a truly extraordinary event, a government secret project or even a hoax perpetrated using, for example, digital photography.

"According to recent surveys, 54% of Americans believe that intelligent extraterrestrial life exists. That footlocker may have provided the proof," Samantha says enthusiastically. She gets up and goes over to the footlocker. She gazes at it, runs her hand over the top and then opens it. Samantha looks inside for a moment and then begins to close the top. She abruptly stops and reopens it. Something is not right with the footlocker. She pokes at a bottom corner. Using her fingernails she tries to pry up a loose piece of wood, but it is too tight. "Do you have a flat screwdriver?" she asks Max excitedly. Seeing her excitement, Max jumps to his feet and heads to the kitchen. "Yeah, why?" he responds. "Just get it!" Samantha commands. Max cannot find a screwdriver, but grabs a butter knife from a drawer in the kitchen and hurries back to Samantha. He hands her the knife and watches in anticipation.

Samantha uses the knife to gently pry open a hidden compartment on the bottom of the footlocker. Inside she finds a 5 x 7 inch manila envelope stamped "U.S. Government Classified – Top Secret". She carefully removes the envelope, turns it over and bends open the metal clasp. Inside Samantha finds three old black and white photos. Her eyes grow open wide and she turns to Max in disbelief. Samantha hands Max the photos. "What the hell is that?" he gasps. "I think that's a good question for Mr. Shepherd," is Samantha's reply.

Just then a knock on the door interrupts them. Max is expecting no one and visitors are infrequent. He glances at Samantha with a confused squint and then walks over to the door. Max checks the position of the baseball bat. Samantha strategically positions herself in a direct line with the door and reaches for her pistol. Max opens the door to find a strange man holding an envelope. "Mr. Shepherd told me I could find Samantha Freeman here," the man says without introducing himself. Samantha rushes to the door. "I'm Samantha Freeman. Who are you" she asks? The man pulls a photo from his pocket and compares it to Samantha. Satisfied, he hands her the envelope and leaves without responding. Samantha walks over to the sofa and sits. Max glances around outside before closing and locking the door.

Max joins Samantha on the sofa as she looks over the envelope. It has no markings of any kind. Samantha opens the envelope and takes out a note she finds inside. It's from Shepherd. "Dr. Shepherd wants to meet with us tomorrow at a farm not far from here," she tells Max. Max stares at her for a moment. "A farm? What the hell! Isn't he being a little overdramatic?" Max complains and adds, "Why don't we just meet at the university or something?" Samantha is puzzled as well, "I don't know, I've known him for over a year and I guess he has a reason," is her explanation. "OK. It's a little strange, but I guess we've got nothing to lose" Max concedes. Samantha is not so sure about that and just nods with a fragile smile.

*   *   *   *   *   *   *

Corvus sits at his desk pondering his problem. While he is not troubled by the death of Mr. Carlson, he is concerned that it might draw unwanted attention to his mission. Max only complicates the issue because Corvus has been unable to determine how much Max knows and what he will do with the information. The real problem may not be Max, but rather Samantha. Corvus reasons that without her, Max may be willing to just sell the material and avoid any conflict. The best solution is to simply eliminate the problem, but that seems risky at the moment.

A slight man dressed neatly in black appears in the doorway to Corvus' office. Corvus glances up to see him and immediately rises. Corvus is obviously surprised to see this visitor. "This is unexpected, but please come in," Corvus says as he rises and steps from behind his desk. His tone is less harsh than normal and he exhibits a modest respect for this man. "You took a great risk in coming here," Corvus lectures the man gently. "The council felt it was important that we speak face to face. They are troubled by the death of Mr. Carlson and question if it was necessary," is the man's response. "It was an unfortunate cost for keeping the faith," Corvus replies unapologetically. "The council is concerned that Mr. Gideon doesn't always consider all his options before employing such an extreme solution," the man lectures Corvus. "Mr. Gideon knows his job and what happens if he fails. This organization has successfully protected the secret for thousands of years and our methods should not be questioned," Corvus replies defensively.

Corvus' organization has no official name but has been referred to throughout the world as the Tutores Fidei or Guardians of the Faith, or just the Tutoribus, or Guardians. The best information available indicates they have some sort of an association with the religions of the world, but only a handful within those religious groups know of the Tutoribus true mission. And, even fewer know the real secret that the Tutoribus are sworn to protect. It is believed the secret is known at only the highest levels of the religious hierarchies.

"If the council is concerned, let them summon me to appear," Corvus argues defiantly. "Remember, we are all are responsible to a higher power for our actions," the man warns Corvus. "That is my burden. Go back to your church and leave me to my work," Corvus instructs the man tersely. The man rises, glares at Corvus and then quietly exits. Corvus takes a deep breath and picks up the file on Max just as Mr. Gideon appears in the doorway. "Build me a profile on Mr. Park. I want to know everything about him, his background, his habits, his schedule and his relationship with Ms. Freeman. I am concerned that Ms. Freeman is becoming too great a risk. Without her, Mr. Park may become inconsequential. Keep an eye on him, but take no action without my orders," are Corvus' instructions to Mr. Gideon. Mr. Gideon nods and disappears into the dark hallway.

Classified documents reportedly indicate a great deal of effort and intelligence resources have been expended investigating the Tutoribus and their secret. Even so, not much is known about the Tutoribus, but evidence suggests that they have existed for thousands of years and even possibly in prehistory under different names. Their roots can be traced all the way back to the Babylonians and some scholars believe even earlier. Many believe the Tutoribus are related to the Mysteries groups that existed in early Greek and Roman culture. Other incarnations throughout history were most likely the Knights of the Sedes Sacrorum in the 15th century whose origins have been traced back to the Babylonians.

Some of these groups have been associated with nefarious activities. According to historical accounts, a number of deaths were attributed to a group called AGLA in France during the 17th and 18th centuries. According to the stories, AGLA killed some priests because it was reported the priests, "revealed too much information". Many believe AGLA gave rise to another group known only as AA - a secret society sworn to protect "The Secret". Finding any significant information regarding AA, like most of these former and current secret societies, is almost impossible. Many historians also believe there are possible connections to the Freemasons and even the Knights of Columbus. Accounts from almost every religious sect describes secret groups granted with extraordinary powers to use whatever means necessary to safeguard the "secret or secret knowledge". These groups believe they are above the law of man and government.

Also according to historical records, it is apparent that these groups are always a step ahead of their adversaries and rarely leave any evidence of their actions. This has led to the belief that such organizations may be responsible for many deaths throughout history otherwise attributed to common criminal acts or natural causes. And, classified intelligence assessments suggest a strong correlation between the deaths of people who reportedly possessed information regarding ETs and the appearance of the Tutoribus.

It is unknown how the Tutoribus recruit their members, but it is believed its agents come from every aspect of personal and professional life including intelligence and law enforcement agencies, which may be why the Tutoribus always seem to have inside information. Whenever anyone gets close to learning the identities of the Tutoribus, they seem to simply disappear. One thing that is consistent about the Tutoribus is that they are always dressed in black. The fact is, that highly classified intelligence assessments identify the Tutoribus are the most likely candidates for the Men in Black, despite the popular notion that the Men in Black are government agents or agents of extraterrestrial origin.

In popular culture and UFO conspiracy theories, the men in black (MIB) are men dressed in black suits who claim to be government agents and who harass or threaten UFO witnesses to force their silence concerning UFO encounters. Some accounts suggest the MIB are, in fact, aliens themselves. The term has also become popular to describe any mysterious men working for unknown organizations as well as various government intelligence and counter-intelligence organizations. The term is used generically within the UFO pop culture for any unusual, menacing or provocative individual whose appearance on the scene can be associated with UFO Phenomena.

It has been determined through ancient texts and architecture that ancient South and North American cultures also possessed information about ETs, and the "secret", but that knowledge was reserved only for the high priests, emperors and kings. Much of this information was recorded in cultural histories, but has been overlooked or misinterpreted as myth by archaeologists and anthropologists. It is also more difficult to trace the Tutoribus within these cultures because of the fragmenting of the civilizations, but evidence for the existence of Tutoribus-like organizations and ET visitors can be found in ancient texts, carvings and in the oral history of Native American, Mesoamerican and South American cultures. Even though archaeologists are now discovering new information being revealed through ancient writings and sculpture, the ultimate secret is still cloaked in secrecy.

Samantha checks her watch. "It's late. I gotta go," she announces. Samantha helps clean up and brings the pizza box to the kitchen. "Pick you up tomorrow morning around 8," she says. "OK, it's a date," Max taunts and braces for her reply. Samantha just smiles and gives him a kiss on the cheek. Max walks her to the front door. She slips on her jacket and heads out the door with a wave. Max watches until Samantha gets into her car and drives away. After a sideways glance around the neighborhood, he closes and locks the door.

Samantha drives down the road. She stops, executes a k-turn and parks on the side of the road giving her a clear view of Max's condo. Samantha pulls out her cell phone and dials the Colonel to request someone to stand watch over Max's condo for the night. She sits in her car watching and waiting. After about 30 minutes, a car appears. It passes her slowly, the driver nods and then parks in front of her. Samantha drives off confident Max is safe for the time being.

Max wonders about Samantha and Shepherd as he cleans up in the kitchen. After all, how well does he really know these people? Samantha seems really nice and Shepherd is a respected professor at the university. But how did Shepherd know Samantha was with him? It all seems a bit odd, but if Max wants answers, he has little choice but to go to the farm. "What the hell? I'm on vacation," he mutters to himself.

FACT VS. FANTASY

DAY THREE

Early the next morning Max gets up and dresses for a cool autumn day. Outside, Samantha returns and the surveillance car drives off as she passes by. She stops in front of Max's condo and taps the horn. Max slips on a jacket, grabs the envelope and heads out the door. He double-times down the steps and jumps into the car with Samantha. "Good morning Ms. Freeman," Max greets her cheerily. "Good morning, Mr. Park" Samantha replies in kind. "I stopped and got some coffee and donuts," she adds as she hands Max a cardboard tray with two cups of coffee and a bag. Max sets the tray on his lap and prepares his coffee as Samantha drives. "So, how well did do you say you know Shepherd?" he asks. "I've been working with him for a year or so. Why?" Samantha questions. "This meeting seems odd to me. And, how did he know where you'd be last night?" is Max's point. "I dunno. I was wondering about that, too. Let's ask him," is Samantha's response.

Max breaks a donut in half and feeds one half to Samantha while she drives. They drive for about an hour and arrive at a farm in a rural area of Massachusetts. They turn down a long dirt drive-way and ride past cows grazing in pastures surrounded by wooded forests. Samantha parks next to a barn hemmed by a corral where a man wearing a cowboy hat, red plaid flannel shirt jacket, and denim jeans is saddling some horses. The man greets them with a wave as they get out of the car. "We're here to see Mr. Shepherd," Samantha announces. Apparently, the man already knows that and informs Max and Samantha that they are going horseback riding.

Max shoots Samantha a quizzical glance over yet another twist in this adventure. Samantha just crinkles her nose and shrugs with a "why not?" kind of attitude. They mount up and ride for about 45 minutes through open fields and over riding trails deep into the woods. They enter a clearing with a small stable and some men who appear to be working in a corral that stands adjacent to the stable. "Time for a break," says their guide. They all dismount and the guide indicates to Max and Samantha they should go inside the building. Max and Samantha peer warily into the stable and then enter cautiously while the guide attends to the horses. The inside of the stable is shadowy and dusty with hay bales stacked about and old leather bridles hanging on the walls. This is all getting a little surreal Max thinks as he looks around the room.

Inside they find Shepherd sipping hot chocolate with three other men. "Good morning Samantha. Good morning, Mr. Park," Shepherd greets them as they enter. "Good morning," Samantha replies. Shepherd offers Samantha and Max a cup of hot chocolate, but they politely decline. Max glances out the door and notices that the guide is now standing watch just outside the entrance. Two of the men that were working in the corral enter behind Max and Samantha and close the door. Max and Samantha stare warily at the men, unsure of who they are and their purpose here.

Shepherd asks them all to sit. They all sit on hay bales scattered throughout the stable. Max shares a hay bale with Samantha. The men sit opposite Max and Samantha in a dim corner of the stable leaving their faces partially obscured by the shadows. "Why is that man out there?" Max asks referring to the guide standing guard. "Do not be concerned. He is there only for your safety. You may leave at any time," Shepherd assures Max. "In fact, I will give you $300 for your material and you may go," Shepherd offers, testing Max's resolve one more time. Max declines with a steely glance and a slow, deliberate shake of his head. Max feels that he has come this far, so might he as well hear what these men have to say.

Shepherd pauses for a moment and then begins by stating that this is a one time opportunity. "Before we begin, please understand that the intention of these gentlemen is to provide answers to your questions regarding Roswell and the existence of intelligent extra-terrestrial life. They will not provide any information that could jeopardize national security," affirms Shepherd. He informs Max and Samantha that if they tell anyone of what they learn, these men can deny any knowledge of the meeting. Shepherds words grow more ominous. Simply having possession of this information could result in criminal charges. And, Shepherd warns, "You risk a visit from some unpleasant people as you know Samantha." Samantha's face tightens. She glances at Max and then acknowledges Shepherd with a nod.

Shepherd introduces the men. The first is Phillip Raymend, USN (Ret.). Raymend was a high-ranking member of Naval Intelligence. Some of his responsibilities included assembling and providing intelligence briefings to the joint chiefs, and preparing intelligence information assessment and reporting for Multi Agency Joint Intelligence Committees (MAJIC). Raymend is a stocky man with a big round face and close-cropped white hair. He is an old sailor's sailor, a Mustang who rose up through the ranks, and who commands respect simply by his presence. Raymend is the kind of man that relaxes with a good cigar and a bottle of Scotch whiskey. His weathered facade hides the mind of a Rhodes Scholar and most of his colleagues wish they knew what he's forgotten when it comes to the field of intelligence. Raymend is one of those guys that you're glad is on our side. He is not a man given to playing frivolous games. If he is here today it is because he has real concerns for the future of his country.

Next is Paul Farmer, an aeronautical engineer with a PhD in astrophysics. Farmer is a retired air force officer who was originally assigned to the USAF Foreign Technology Division (FTD) at Wright Patterson Air force Base in Dayton, Ohio, renamed the National Air and Space Intelligence Center (NASIC), and also worked for DARPA (Defense Advanced Research Projects Agency). The FTD was the precursor to the NASIC which is now the United States Air Force unit for analyzing intelligence regarding foreign air and space forces, weapons, and systems. NASIC's assessments of aerospace technology's performance characteristics, capabilities, and vulnerabilities are used to define national security and defense policies and programs. DARPA is the U.S. Department of Defense agency responsible for the development of emerging technologies for use by the military.

Farmer is an average man with a receding hairline whose face appears frozen in a permanent scowl. But, he is not your average geek. He is an accomplished aeronautical engineer with a library of patents to his credit and has worked in an enterprise more secret than the Lockheed Skunk Works. He speaks in technical tongues that few can understand, but when he speaks everyone listens. He has reversed engineered most of the world's foreign aircraft and space technology. If alien technology were available he would be one of the first to have seen it. If it flies, Farmer would know about it.

Area 51 was a second home to him through his work with the Red Hats, the 4477th Test and Evaluation Squadron responsible for the testing and evaluation of "acquired" foreign aircraft and technology.

Sitting alongside farmer is Dr. John Walker who has a PhD in psychology and was a linguist for the Air Intelligence Agency and subsequently the Air Force Intelligence, Surveillance and Reconnaissance Agency (AFISRA), re-designated as the 25th Air Force in 2007. His responsibilities included interviewing defectors and debriefing POWs as well as translating and analyzing intercepted communications. Walker is thin and quiet with a narrow face and curly salt and pepper hair. He is fastidious in his appearance and even at a meeting in a dusty stable is wearing a button down shirt with a neck tie. Walker's quiet presence is exactly what one would expect of a psychologist. Language is second nature to Walker and he speaks nine. Walker also has a special talent. He has been described as a human polygraph and has been a leader in psi (parapsychology) research. His friends sometimes call him the Oracle for his proven psychic abilities.

Psi or Parapsychology is concerned with the investigation of paranormal and psychic phenomena which includes telepathy, precognition, clairvoyance, and psycho kinesis. Most people believe that parapsychology research is conducted by private institutions and typically funded through "private" donations. And, the subject rarely appears in mainstream science journals. However, an official CIA paper written by Gerald K. Haines, the historian of the *National Reconnaissance Office* (NRO) reveals, 'There is a Defense Intelligence Agency (DIA) Psychic Center and the NSA (National Security Agency) studies parapsychology. In addition, the military, especially the U.S. Navy, have issued a number of contracts to study psi. The DIA is an intelligence service of the United States specializing in defense and military intelligence.

Then there is Rick Tucker who was a technical advisor on special projects for the U.S. government. He holds an M.S. degree in software engineering. He worked for the Air Intelligence Agency and DARPA as well as a number of highly regarded defense contractors as part of carve-out projects. A "carve-out" or "swine" project is a top secret project that has been "carved out" of a government military or intelligence organization and assigned to a private corporation. Sometimes the private corporation has been created by an intelligence organization as a cover to shield the project from FOIA (Freedom of Information Act) requests. Tucker's specialty was C4 (Command, Control, Communications and Computers) intelligence in the areas of cyber systems data and communications security, verification, encryption and forensics. Tucker is tall and graying around the temples. By all appearances he is just an affable businessman. He is personable and articulate with a keen sense of humor. But in the shadows of cyber space he is described as a wolf who demands excellence from himself and anyone with whom he works. He has also been described as both brilliant and formidable by his colleagues and adversaries alike, and can be impatient with people who don't possess his talent. He is well aware that the next war could be fought in cyber space and will do whatever is necessary to ensure his country is prepared.

Lastly, Ken Hartman was the Director of Special Projects, more specifically, carve-out or swine projects for the Air Intelligence Agency with whom Walker and Tucker worked. Hartman has an MBA and a Master's degree in Economics. He is a slight, quiet man with an angular face and round, wire-rimmed glasses. In addition to intelligence gathering and assessment, one of Hartman's projects was to create a private holding company whose wholly-owned corporations generate revenue for the black budget. These private "corporations" avoid scrutiny of the GAO (General Accounting Office) and are immune from FOI (Freedom of Information Act) inquiries.

Shepherd goes on to explain that these men know just about all there is to know regarding the subject of ETs. Their work afforded them the highest level security clearance which provided access to one of the most highly classified secrets in the history of mankind – the existence of intelligent ET life and its presence on Earth. "They know more than most presidents and have agreed to share some of this info with you," Shepherd asserts. Shepherd was referring to the fact that not all presidents were, or are, aware of the UFO and ET situation. Eisenhower, Kennedy, Nixon, Reagan and both Bush's were reportedly the few.

There is no need for Presidents or legislators to know, and the feeling among military and intelligence analysts is that most cannot be trusted with the information. "The politicians know only what we tell them and we don't tell them everything regardless of what committee they sit on," Raymend boasts insolently. "And the current administration?" Samantha inquires. "The current administration is the greatest threat to our country in its history," Raymend grumbles. "Easy, Phil, it was just a birth certificate" Tucker jibes him. "Yeah, Tuck? Well, it was just an election," Raymend snarls back. The implications being the two are connected and there was nefarious activity on both counts. Tucker glares at Raymend momentarily. That's definitely a conversation for another time Max thinks, but he's just trying to deal with the moment. Shepherd steps in, "Gentlemen, we have other issues to address at the moment." Shepherd turns to Max and Samantha and asks, "Do either of you have questions before we begin?"

"Yeah, why tell ME all this?" Max asks provocatively. "Why not? You found the evidence on Roswell, so you already know some of the story. And we all believe it's time to tell our side. We attended a UFO conference. Thought it would be fun, but what we heard disturbed us. OK?" Raymend responds aggressively. Shepherd steps in with a more moderate tone. "We checked you out and decided that you and Ms. Freeman can be trusted with the truth. The burden will be yours," Shepherd informs them. "What burden?" Max asks, his forehead furrowed in a display of confusion. "Knowledge most would prefer not to know. You will understand better after. Any other questions before we begin?" Shepherd reiterates. "How did you know where I would be last night?" is Samantha's question. "You will understand after," Shepherd says again with a wry smile.

"You would like to know more about Roswell," Shepherd states as his way of confirming Max and Samantha's commitment one last time. Despite the ominous warnings, Max and Samantha nod affirmatively. "May I see the documents," Shepherd asks Max. Max hands Shepherd the envelope and Shepherd passes it on to Raymend. The newly discovered photos flutter to the ground as Raymend slips the papers out of the envelope. Shepherd picks up the photos and studies them. His brow arches and he glances at Max and Samantha with a sly smile. Raymend examines the carbons and paper, and then passes them on to Farmer.

Raymend is the first to speak. He begins by revealing that Roswell happened pretty much as reported, but there are a few facts missing from the official report. His tone is even and matter of fact. As Raymend speaks, the others nod in agreement. Raymend concedes that there was a Project Mogul balloon involved in the Roswell crash just as the Air Force reported, but the fact is, that it was not alone in the skies that evening. Raymend asserts that during the Roswell investigation, the military determined that an ET craft was in close proximity to the Project Mogul balloon when the alien craft crashed. Project Mogul was a nuclear test monitoring system using a special radar-equipped, weather balloon-based apparatus. Apparently, the ET was examining the balloon and its radar reflectors during a violent thunderstorm when the balloon's reflectors were struck by lightning. The discharge caused by the lightning strike disrupted the electromagnetic fields generated by the ET craft and it crashed, or rather bounced off the ground causing the large furrow in the pasture at the first site. The balloon disintegrated and its debris mixed with debris from the ET craft on the field.

The ET craft managed to get airborne again briefly, but crashed up-range in the mountains west of Roswell at a second site where an almost complete but damaged ET craft was reportedly discovered amidst the rocks and boulders. Farmer notes that the craft was not crescent-shaped as rumored, but rather elliptical or more egg-shaped. He postulates that the crash damage may have made it appear crescent-shaped to some witnesses which lead to early speculation that the craft might have been a Nazi Horton HO 229 flying wing. But, that speculation was quickly dismissed upon detailed examination of the craft. Farmer also confirms that the craft was made of an incredibly light-weight material just as Brazel and Major Marcel described. The material was so strong that it was believed the damage was not likely caused by the impact with the ground, but rather by an internal explosion generated by the impact.

Raymend continues to reveal, "Alien entities were found at the second crash site, but it was later determined that these were biologically engineered machines or androids." According to Raymend, these creatures were not the actual ETs. Subsequent analysis revealed they were entities who appeared specifically designed for space travel. These creatures had large fluid-filled heads to cushion their brains against gravitational forces. Their large, dark eyes were designed to adapt to the various lighting conditions they might encounter throughout their space travel. These creatures had no digestive system making it unnecessary to store and consume food, and no lungs to require any type of respiration. Their small, about 4 foot tall, slight body was, again, to allow them to easily adapt to varying gravitational forces. "The conclusion was that these creatures which have been referred to as the 'Greys,' were not actual aliens but biological creations of an advanced race, which may explain their insensitivity to human suffering," Raymend reports. He then discloses that these creatures were called "Goblins" in the original classified reports, but this was later refined to "Biologically Engineered Entities" and the creatures were code named BEEs. "The approach to using the BEEs is similar to our system of drones and UAVs, but much more sophisticated. As our technology advances, future U.S. aircraft will rely heavily on unmanned aircraft flown by designs not unlike the BEEs," Farmer hints.

There is more. Raymend contends that three, six-inch diameter, opaque, crystalline spheres that apparently use some form of light energy to store information, were also found in the craft. It took years, but eventually some of the information was deciphered when a major U.S. computer manufacturer was able to synthesize the storage and retrieval process. Raymend confirms that Major Marcel was ordered to participate in the Roswell cover-up story for the sake of national security and assures Max and Samantha there was no direct contact with the actual ETs at that time. This seems to answer Max's questions about Marcel and his promotion.

Raymend also contends that the reason no official information has ever been discovered regarding Roswell was that key information was coded and all records classified Top Secret at the highest levels. "It was directed that there be no references to 'Roswell, Flying Discs, Disks, Saucers, or aliens', or the craft in any reports or communications regarding the incident making such information intentionally difficult to track," is Raymend's explanation. Raymend reveals that the code name for the incident was "Thunderhead" and the craft was to be referred to as the "item". Raymend stresses that absolute secrecy was the order of the day. "If a witness says his life was threatened should he reveal any info, I believe it," Raymend confesses.

The CIC (Counter Intelligence Corps) was responsible for the security surrounding the Roswell incident. The official mission of the CIC was the detection, neutralization and/or destruction of espionage, sedition and sabotage against the US Army. At the end of World War II, CIC personnel were successful in an operation called "Paper Clip" that recruited German Rocket Scientists for America before the Soviets "conscripted" them. This action aided in the success of the U.S. rocket development program and resultant space program. The CIC actively conducted intelligence and counter intelligence activities during the Cold War, Viet Nam War and Korean War. The CIC was heavily involved in the security for the Normandy Invasion and development of the Atomic Bomb among other projects, as well as in the cover up of the Roswell Incident. "They were extremely successful in protecting America against its enemies; however, their techniques were often ruthless and intimidating even to American citizens," Raymend remarks like a person who had observed such techniques firsthand.

"The truth is that the Roswell information was so highly classified that few people were even aware of its existence. By now, most of those that knew of the reports have died and taken the secrets to the grave. You, Mr. Park have found the only remaining evidence to this event that we are aware of," Raymend explains. Raymend pauses and sips his hot chocolate as Max and Samantha ponder his words. Raymend can see their faces are twisted in confusion, or rather disbelief. A moment passes. Samantha breaks the silence. "What is the deposition?" she inquires. "I think Mr. Walker can best explain that," Shepherd replies as he turns the conversation over to Walker. Hartman hands the documents back to Shepherd, removes his glasses and cleans them. Max notices that Hartman has done this a number of times throughout the discussion. Definitely quirky, but that seems to reflect the theme of this whole bizarre experience Max thinks.

Shepherd slips one carbon out from the others and hands it to Samantha. "What you hold in your hand is a statement taken from one of the occupants of the Roswell craft prior to its 'death,' explaining the purpose of their mission. Few knew of this and all copies were supposedly destroyed," Walker states. "Mission?" Max inquires curiously. Walker exchanges a glance with Shepherd as if seeking direction. Shepherd nods his encouragement with a thin smile. Walker still appears reluctant but continues, "Monitor the earth and its inhabitants, and provide the information to an ET council of scientific and cultural experts for analysis. For what purpose, we're not sure." Max shakes his head in disbelief over Walker's answer. Shepherd holds up one of the photos, a Grey alien. "This is one of the occupants," he says. Samantha shakes her head slowly and tries to comprehend what she is hearing.

"I don't believe it. You're telling me this really happened and no one else knows about it?" Max challenges Walker. "There are a few like you, but most of the Roswell information was lost or destroyed. Very few in military and intelligence know the details of Roswell. We suspect spiritual leaders have known of ET for ages, but disguise it in religious myth," is Walker's explanation. "And, of course there were others like Wernhner von Braun, Kelly Johnson and Ben Rich," Farmer adds. "But there is something more. Something that even we don't know," Raymend interjects. Max jumps to his feet. He screws up his face and shakes his head. "OK. This is a gag. You got me!" Max exclaims. He glances at Samantha but her etched expression suggests she is as bewildered as Max. He glances at each of the men for a sign he has exposed their ruse, but they remain stone-faced. Max takes a deep breath and sits back down struck with the growing possibility this is all true.

"Who are 'They,' and how did they get here?" Samantha asks hoping for some kind of scientific corroboration for this story. "Who they are and where they come from is unimportant," Shepherd responds ambiguously. Raymend commandeers the conversation, possibly to save Shepherd from further explanation, and points out that it is a closely guarded secret, on the part of the ETs, how many actual ETs visit Earth. "Mostly it is their biological proxies, the BEEs. But I would not be surprised that people interact more than we realize with ETs without even knowing it," Raymend adds.

He explains that when it was determined we were dealing with two distinct entities, code names were created to differentiate between them. The actual aliens who created the BEEs were originally designated as a "Non-Human Alien Species" and code named "Zyrans" in early classified reports. This was a reference to the fictional planet, Zyra, from the 1933 science fiction novel, *When Worlds Collide*, by Philip Wylie and Edwin Balmer. "We didn't know who they were or where they came from and, in effect, worlds were colliding. This was changed to "Nomads" in subsequent reports, but they are sometimes also referred to as "Tourists," Raymend asserts. He clarifies that the names were created to avoid any direct reference to aliens or "space men" that could provide easy detection of such information in classified documents. Raymend does not know the reason for the change of terms from Zyrans to Nomads. He also notes that in the late 1970's it was not uncommon to hear the Nomads referred to as "ET" in conversation, using the term popularized by the movie of the same name. But that reference was forbidden in any official written documents, classified or otherwise.

Raymend goes on to reveal that the Nomads say their mission is to study the Universe and life within it. According to the Nomads, life exists on a broad scale throughout the Universe. "It is our understanding that we are working with one specific alien race," he states. Raymend also reveals that the Nomads are similar in form to humans, but have an advanced physiology and intelligence. And, their culture is millions of years old, even though they mark time differently. "I don't know how," Raymend adds, but explains based on the data that has been collected it is apparent Nomads have been here for many thousands of years and likely influenced early civilizations in ways that are we are just beginning to understand.

"Mr. Farmer, can you explain how they got here?" Shepherd asks. Farmer hesitates as he glances at the other men. He agreed to participate, but now is not so sure this is a good idea. "Paul," Raymend growls sternly, his eyes fixed intensely on Farmer. A moment passes. "OK. I can tell you what we've learned, but it's still way beyond our level of comprehension," Farmer replies tersely.

According to Farmer, space travel is achieved by traversing dimensional barriers. Dimensional travel capability can be compared to passing through the sound barrier, but much more complex and apparently requires deceleration rather than acceleration. The manipulation of electromagnetic fields (EMF) and gravitational waves appear to be the secret. Stars and planets are all sources of electromagnetic fields and generate gravitational forces. The ETs have the ability to manipulate those forces to push and pull objects through space, as well as generate energy. It is like using a transformer or voltage regulator to boost or reduce power, but in this case, using ambient electromagnetic fields and gravitational waves, which can be quite subtle. "We have observed one application is their neutralization of gravitational forces yielding an antigravity capability for unrestricted flight" Farmer adds.

As an engineer, Max is familiar with the concept of electromagnetic fields. An electromagnetic field (EMF) is a physical field produced by the interaction of electrically charged objects. The objects within the electromagnetic field possess either a positive or negative electrical charge. A simple electric motor produces an electromagnetic field when it operates because of its use of electricity to spin magnets with positive and negative poles to generate power. Physicists believe electromagnetic fields can extend indefinitely throughout space. One of noted physicist's James Clerk Maxwell's equations suggests that a changing magnetic field produces an electric field and alternate equation indicates that a changing electric field produces a magnetic field. An electromagnetic wave results from the two processes producing a steady flow of radiated energy that can travel far from the source. All stars, planets, and cosmic gases emit various forms of electromagnetic radiation (EM) or positively and negatively charged particles that can generate electromagnetic fields. EM Radiation includes the visible light that comes from a lamp in your house as well as the radio waves that emanate from a radio station, for example. The other types of EM radiation that make up the electromagnetic spectrum include microwaves, infrared light, ultraviolet light, X-rays and gamma-rays. In other words, just about every object in space generates EMFs and those electromagnetic fields travel throughout space.

The concept of gravitational waves is much more complex and this is new to Max. Gravitational waves are ripples in the curvature of space-time that spread throughout the Universe as waves. Gravitational waves are produced in certain gravitational interactions and travel outward from the source, such as a planet or star. Albert Einstein predicted the existence of gravitational waves based on his theory of general relativity, which suggested gravitational waves transport energy as gravitational radiation. Conversely, gravitational waves do not exist in the Newtonian theory of gravitation; the old apple falling from the tree on Newton's head. Newtonian theory assumes that gravitational interactions propagate at infinite speed resulting in more of a constant field of energy. Nevertheless, Farmer's statements add a whole new perspective to the application of this energy. What Farmer is saying is that somehow, the Nomads use this energy to "surf" the Universe.

Despite current theories about multiple universes, Farmer states that we are told by the Nomads that there is only one universe, but there are multiple dimensions within that Universe. He alleges the Nomads have indicated that the Universe is like a sponge, made up of a solid portion as well as empty spaces or pores, which our science is just beginning to perceive as dark matter and energy. Time exists only in the solid state and not in the holes or empty spaces. The empty spaces are actually separate dimensions of dark matter. There are many dimensions within the Universe each with various levels or planes. The human condition of death is a dimensional experience in a plane that requires only energy and thus the concept of existence can vary by dimension. Farmer points out that, "Apparently, there are some dimensions where you don't want to go because it can permanently alter your existence." He continues to explain that dimensions can expand and contract thus affecting other dimensions and universal space.

Farmer continues his lecture. He provides an example by suggesting Max and Samantha try thinking of a 3 dimensional matrix where an infinite arrangement of the cells can represent different dimensions. Thus it is possible to have one dimension within another, or a dimension made up of two dimensions even though each of the dimensions also exists separately. And, dimensions can be made up of multiple planes imperceptible to the others. Farmer can see the glazed look in the eyes of Max and Samantha. "I don't completely understand it either. I'm just telling you what we've been told," Farmer confesses. "The science is still way beyond our comprehension which is why we cannot duplicate their technology," he concedes contritely.

According to classified reports, the Nomads have shared some technology with us for study but have not provided any operational "manuals" or engineering details. "We suspect they may have shared this same technology with foreign governments as well," Farmer reveals. He also explains that most of the actionable knowledge gained from the Nomads is applied first to defense applications, but some like light wave and laser optical technology in addition to computer chip processor and data storage technology has already made its way to the commercial markets. Farmer discloses that some major universities and private corporations working on government projects are researching technological concepts garnered from the Nomads, but are unaware from where the technological innovation came.

"So, all those stories I've read about UFOs are true," Max states for confirmation. "Some are, but most are just misidentifications or plain fantasy. People tend to let their imaginations run wild," Hartman responds shaking his head in contempt. "There's a fair amount of disinformation out there as well. The Nomads are aware of our UFO culture and may even be involved in some way. We also suspect some of the so-called 'ufologists' are actually Tutoribus, a religious group sworn to keep ETs a secret by spreading disinformation and eroding the credibility of legitimate UFO researchers," Tucker adds. This is the first Max has heard of the Tutoribus. He turns to Samantha, "Are those the people?" he asks. She nods affirmatively. "The aforementioned are not so nice people," Shepherd comments.

Hartman continues, "1952 Washington DC, Exeter, the nuke sites at Minot, Malmstrom and Benwaters air force bases, for example, are all real encounters." "And, there is a growing debate by scientists as to whether or not some of the structures found on Mars are natural," Tucker interjects. Max remembers these names from his research. The 1952 Washington DC "flap" was a series of UFO reports that were accompanied by radar contacts at three separate Washington DC area airports as well as aircraft and ground visual confirmations. According to reports, there were seven to 12 objects observed on radar moving as fast as 7000 mph. The sightings occurred on two different occasions a week apart.

The 1952 incident was also known as the Washington National Airport Sightings. The most publicized sightings took place on consecutive weekends, July 19 and 20 and July 26 and 27, in 1952. The unidentified objects, described as bright orange lights, flew over the White House and the United States Capitol, causing Andrews Air Force Base to scramble jet interceptors in response. The resulting country-wide headlines regarding the events precipitated the formation of the CIA Robertson Panel. The Robertson Panel was a scientific committee which convened in January of 1953 and was headed by Howard P. Robertson, PH.D, a physicist and mathematician. The Panel was assembled based on a recommendation to the Intelligence Advisory Committee (IAC) in December of 1952 stemming from a CIA review of the U.S. Air Force's Project Blue Book investigation into unidentified flying objects. The CIA review was a response to increasingly widespread reports of unidentified flying objects, especially in the Washington, D.C. area during the summer of 1952. A number of criticisms have been leveled at the Robertson panel and its conclusion that further study of UFOs was not indicated. In particular, many felt that the panel's examination of the phenomena was relatively perfunctory and its conclusions essentially predetermined by the earlier CIA review of the UFO enigma. Based on what Farmer is saying, the criticism was justified because a decision was made, for whatever reason, to withhold the truth from the public.

At the time, the U.S. Air Force alleged that a temperature inversion, in which a layer of warm, moist air covering a layer of cool, dry air closer to the ground, had caused radar signals to bend and give false returns. The problem with that explanation was that the Washington objects were actually seen by witnesses on the ground and in the air as well as by pilots. And, according to witnesses, the targets disappeared when jet interceptors entered the area and reappeared after they left.

The 'Exeter Incident' occurred in September of 1966 when Norman Muscarello, two Police officers and other witnesses observed strange lights in Exeter, New Hampshire. Cars reportedly stalled and restarted by themselves. An effect we now know to be caused by EMFs. As Muscarello walked along Highway 150 late one night, he noticed five flashing red lights in the nearby woods. The lights illuminated the woods and a nearby farmhouse. As the lights moved towards him, Muscarello became terrified and hid in a ditch. The lights moved away and hovered near the farmhouse momentarily, eventually moving back into the woods. Muscarello ran to the farmhouse, pounded on the door and yelled for help, but no one answered. He ran back onto Route 150, forced an oncoming car to stop, and convinced the couple in the car to drive him to the Exeter police station.

Muscarello blurted his story to police officer Reginald Toland, who was working the night desk at the Exeter police station. Toland, who knew Muscarello personally, was impressed by Muscarello's obvious fear and agitation. Toland radioed police officer Eugene Bertrand, Jr., who had earlier in the evening reported speaking with a distressed woman he found sitting in her car on Highway 108. The woman told Bertrand, that a "huge object with flashing red lights" had followed her car for 12 miles and stopped over her car, causing it to stall, before flying away. After returning to the police station and hearing Muscarello's story, Bertrand decided to drive back to the farm with Muscarello to investigate. They observed nothing unusual from Bertrand's patrol car; however, when they approached the woods where Muscarello had first seen the objects, horses in a nearby corral became excited and began kicking their stalls and making loud, frightened noises. Dogs in the area also began howling.

Bertrand and Muscarello observed a large object slowly rise up from the woods. Bertrand described the UFO as "this huge, dark object as big as a barn, with red flashing lights." The object moved slowly towards them, swaying back and forth like a leaf fluttering gently in the breeze. Bertrand grabbed Muscarello, and both men ran back to the patrol car where Bertrand radioed for assistance. Exeter police officer, David Hunt, was dispatched. While waiting for Hunt to arrive, Betrand and Muscarello watched the object as it hovered 100 feet away and at an altitude of about 100 feet. The object rocked back and forth and the pulsating red lights flashed in sequence. Hunt finally arrived on the scene and also observed the strange object until it flew away over the woods and disappeared. The three men drove back to the Exeter police station and immediately filed separate reports describing in detail what they had observed. The Exeter incident remains listed as unexplained by the United States Air Force even though the November/December 2011 edition of *Skeptical Inquirer* Magazine suggested that the sighting was just an Air Force airborne refueling tanker. However, this was actually an old explanation that was dismissed by the Air Force in 1965. Was this because the Air Force already knew the answer, Max wonders? Farmer seemingly answers the question by revealing, "The Nomads subsequently conceded this event was caused by an equipment malfunction."

The incursions at the Air Force bases are even more disturbing. In 1967 at Malmstron Air Force Base, Montana, Lt. Col. Robert Salas stated that 20 nuclear Minuteman missiles went offline in the silos when guards reported a glowing object hovering over the gates of the base. According to the official report by Brigadier General Wilman D. Barnes, the Deputy Director for Operations of the National Military Command Center (NMCC), Malmstrom AFB in Montana received seven radar returns on the height-finder radar. At the same time, witnesses on the ground observed lights in the sky over the base. However, a cross-check with the FAA (Federal Aviation Administration) mysteriously revealed no aircraft within 100 miles of the area. Military radar also tracked the objects over Lewistown, Montana at a speed of seven knots (about 8 mph). Two F-106 Fighters from the 24th NORAD Region were scrambled to intercept the targets. At the time, personnel at Malmstrom AFB and Strategic Air Command (SAC) missile sites K1, K3, L3 and L6 were reporting seeing lights in the sky. The objects turned west and increased speed to 150 knots (about 172 mph). The personnel at the four SAC sites reported observing that when the F-106's arrived in the area, the objects extinguished their lights, and turned them back on upon the F-106's departure. Official USAF reports exist for this event and similar events that took place at Minot AFB, in North Dakota.

On March 5, 1967, Air Defense Command radar tracked an unidentified target descending over the Minuteman missile silos of the 91st Strategic Missile Wing at Minot AFB, ND. Base security teams quickly converged on the area and reported seeing a metallic, disc-shaped craft ringed with bright, flashing lights moving slowly over the base. The disc stopped and hovered about 500 feet off the ground as security police watched in awe. Suddenly the object began moving again and circled directly over the launch control facility. F-106 fighter-interceptors were standing by on the flight line, reportedly waiting impatiently for an order from NORAD to scramble. When the order was not forthcoming, base operations decided on their own to scramble the interceptors. At exactly the moment the fighters launched, witnesses reported the UFO climbed straight up and streaked away at incredible speed. Is there a profound reason NORAD had not issued a scramble order?

In the United Kingdom in December of 1980, radar screens at Royal Air Forces (RAF) Wattonin, Norfolk showed an uncorrelated object which suddenly appeared in the vicinity of the Rendlesham Forest in Suffolk. The object was also tracked on radar at Bentwaters RAF, which was located north of the forest, and at Woodbridge located just south of the forest. Both bases were reported to have a large stockpile of nuclear weapons and Woodbridge was the home of the U.S. Air Force 67th Aerospace Rescue and Recovery Squadron, a special operations unit accountable only to the U.S. Department of Defense in Washington, D.C. The sightings occurred over a period of several nights and were confirmed in official reports by Lt. Col. Charles Halt, the Bentwaters Deputy Base Commander as well as a number of Air Force personnel who were sent to investigate the objects. "The reports describe an anomalous craft and a number of electromagnetic effects," Farmer remarks.

The extraordinary events of Woodbridge/Bentwaters began with the sighting of a glowing object by three security guards patrolling the twin bases. After requesting permission to check out the strange sightings, they followed the lights into the forest. Their initial presumption was that a military or commercial aircraft had made a crash landing. The guards were shocked and frightened to find a saucer-like craft. The craft was absolutely silent and had a surface that felt like smooth pebbled glass.

Colonel Halt, called out on the second night of the sightings, was one of a group of senior officers to pursue the strange, glowing object through the forest. He would become a key figure in the Rendlesham investigation. During the investigation in the woods, he made an audio cassette of his experience for subsequent analysis. Col. Halt still has the tape recordings and notes he made during the events, and copies of the official reports that were submitted to the Air Force and RAF. "Classified reports suggest this was an ET drone, but that has never been revealed publicly or to any of the participants, or the even British government," Farmer states, and adds, "While the Nomads acknowledge these events, they have offered no explanations." "We believe they are routinely assessing our capabilities," Raymend submits.

"Hey Phil, I understand that the Navy has a secret UFO database. Can you tell us anything about Shag Harbor?" Hartman asks. Raymend glances inquisitively at Tucker. Tucker puts up his hands and smirks, indicating he didn't spill the secret. Raymend hesitates.

The Shag Harbor incident occurred in October of 1967 in Shag Harbor, a small fishing village located at the southern tip of Nova Scotia. This incident involved a USO (Unidentified Submerged Object) and is considered to be one of the best documented UFO events in the history of the UFO phenomenon. According to the reports, witnesses watched four orange lights flashing in sequence as they descended on a 45 degree angle toward the sea. The witnesses stated that the lights did not crash into the water, but appeared to float on the surface about a half mile from the shore. Witnesses believed they were watching an aircraft crash landing into the sea and immediately reported it to the Royal Canadian Mounted Police (RCMP).

RCMP Constable Ronald Pound had already observed the lights as he drove down Highway 3 en route to Shag Harbor. Pound believed the lights were attached to one aircraft that he estimated to be about 60 feet long. Constable Pound, accompanied by Police Corporal Victor Werbieki, Constable Ron O'Brien, and some local residents ran to the shoreline to get a closer look. The witnesses reported seeing a yellow light that appeared to be slowly moving across the water, leaving a yellowish foam in its wake. They watched until it apparently dipped below the surface of the icy North Atlantic waters.

Canadian Coast Guard cutters and local boats rushed to the scene, but by the time they arrived, the light was gone. However, they reported seeing the yellow foam on the surface of the water, indicating that something had been there and apparently submerged. According to reports, surface vessels and divers searched the waters for several days but found nothing.

A subsequent investigation indicated that the divers and other witnesses reported the object left Shag Harbor and traveled underwater about 25 miles to a place called Government Point near a submarine detection base. The object was detected on sonar and Navy ships were positioned on the surface above it. After a couple of days, a second USO reportedly joined the first. Common belief at the time was that the second craft had arrived to assist the first. After about a week of observing the two UFOs, a Russian submarine was detected entering the Canadian waters. According to the report, it was at this time the two USOs proceeded underwater to the Gulf of Maine, pursued by the Navy, and then surfaced and shot away into the skies.

Raymend glances around the room as if deciding on how to respond to the question. He sighs and reveals that, "Shag Harbor was a Broken Arrow; a Soviet Broken Arrow." Except for Tucker, the other men seemed surprised. "A Broken Arrow is an accidental loss of nuclear weapons or nuclear components like in a plane crash, for example," Farmer explains to Max and Samantha. "Despite all the denials, the U.S. Navy was involved. The Russian sub was too late and we recovered the Soviet technology. Much of what the witnesses reported was an orchestrated diversion. You can understand the reason for all the secrecy," Raymend confides. The men nod. Max notices that while Raymend has explained the Shag Harbor incident, he did not address Hartman's statement about a secret Navy UFO database, and Max believes this is not an oversight. But, no one seems to want to push the issue.

"There have been a number of military base incursions, both UFO and USO, that have never been disclosed and remain classified. Similar activity continues to this day, but the information is highly classified and compartmented," Raymend adds as perhaps a subtle acknowledgement regarding the Navy database. "The activity you do not hear about is much greater than that which you do," Walker remarks. He explains that over the years he has debriefed many pilots from the U.S. and around the world regarding their experiences with unidentified aircraft that we knew were the Nomads, but that information was never shared with those pilots or foreign governments in such cases. "I'm sure it's no big surprise, but NASA has its own files that I understand are quite significant," Raymend adds. He goes on to explain that his involvement was limited, but any reports from NASA with potential national security implications passed through his office. "From the very beginning of the space program our astronauts were being observed by the Nomads. At first, the space crews found it disquieting, but now it is accepted as routine. The International Space Station has presented a delicate situation. I don't know just how much is shared with the international crew in the case of actual sightings, which are being publicly trivialized as misidentifications of celestial events and space debris to maintain security," Raymend reports. "I suspect it is all a cat and mouse game. We know other governments are aware of the Nomads and likely communicate with them as well," Farmer remarks.

"The flying triangles! What about the flying triangles?" Max exclaims. Farmer rolls his eyes and the others glance at him and laugh. "That's a bad subject for Paul. He's tired of hearing about the triangles," explains Hartman who smiles for the first time. "Let it go! For the last time, they're not ET," growls an exasperated Farmer. The room becomes silent and all eyes are on Farmer as they restrain their amusement. Farmer takes a deep breath and explains that in the 1980's the so-called Hudson Valley sightings were actually a military drone-based, electronic surveillance and countermeasures project. During the height of the activity, literally thousands of witnesses, including police officers and scientists, observed triangular or boomerang-shaped objects, and many photos and videos were taken. The "siege" generated over 7,000 documented sightings of a boomerang-shaped craft or crafts moving silently through the sky over New York and Connecticut between 1982 and 1995. Nevertheless, the U.S. government showed little interest in the reports, perhaps a tell-tale sign the objects were not a mystery. According to Farmer, flight testing was subsequently repeated around the world in places like Belgium and even Phoenix, AZ. And, the sightings continue to this day around the world.

The purpose of the project was to test a digital reconnaissance and aerial global observation network. Farmer alleges the project involved technology from some of the leading defense contractors like Raytheon, General Electric, Northrup, Lockheed and United Technologies as well as the U.S. Air Force and NASA. Where they got the inspiration for this technology was a secret, but there were rumors. "Basically, this is a sensor array, but is much more. It can actually "sniff" out electronic signals, chemical signatures and even human beings, as well as track physical movements of assets and intercept all data and voice communications," Farmer reveals. This project was classified Top Secret and compartmented under the control of operations KEYHOLE and subsequently ENDSEAL.

Farmer concedes that the whole incident in the 1980's was the result of poor decision making. Normally these aircraft would not display navigational lights except a decision, a bad decision in hindsight, was made to test over densely populated areas to assess the technology's true capability, and navigational lights were deemed necessary. Without the lights the whole project may have gone un-noticed. This information has never been declassified because of ongoing research and development. "Have you seen the Northrup-Grumman TV commercial showcasing their advanced technology? Did you notice the triangle shadow on the clouds in the last scene, yet there is no visible aircraft," Farmer submits rhetorically as evidence supporting his assertions. He also suggests that Lockheed-Martin offers a commercial version of the sensing technology, called Dragon, but not as sophisticated as the classified military technology.

According to the five men, the infamous Kecksburg, Pennsylvania event was actually the recovery of a U.S. spy satellite through Project Moondust. The Kecksburg UFO incident, as it has been called, occurred in December of 1965, at Kecksburg, Pennsylvania. According to reports, a large, brilliant fireball was seen by thousands of people as it streaked over the Detroit, Michigan and the Windsor, Ontario, Canada area dropping hot metal debris over Michigan and northern Ohio. Witnesses reported the hot debris triggered grass fires and sonic booms were reported in the Pittsburgh metropolitan area. It was generally reported by the press to be a meteor after authorities dismissed explanations such as a plane crash, errant missile test, or reentering satellite debris.

However, eyewitnesses in the small village of Kecksburg claimed something odd crashed in the woods. One boy said he saw the object land and his mother, seeing what she described as blue smoke in the woods, alerted authorities. Local volunteer fire fighters rushed to the scene and reported finding an object in the shape of an acorn and about as large as a Volkswagen Beetle with writing resembling Egyptian hieroglyphs on a band around the base. Witnesses also reported that the United States Army arrived and quickly secured the area, ordering civilians away, and then removed an object on a flatbed truck. The official military report indicated they searched the woods and found "absolutely nothing."

Farmer explains the Kecksburg "craft" was one of a series of spy satellites designed by General Electric to gather surveillance data and then return the information to Earth using a re-entry vehicle. At the time, satellite to ground communication links were unreliable and insecure, so any sensitive information gathered via satellite had to be sent back to earth by means of a re-entry vehicle or aircraft. This was the reason for the U2 and SR71 spy plane programs. All the secrecy surrounding the Kecksburg event was simply because the U.S. government did not want the Soviets to know we had such capability and were conducting such surveillance. "Although given the publicity they must have known about the touch down," Farmer remarks. Okay, Max can accept all of that. It is no surprise to him that the government has secret projects that people can mistake for UFOs. Finally they have moved back from the world of bizarre to just eerie he thinks. But, Samantha just has to stoke the fire of bizarre.

"Do the Nomads communicate with us?" Samantha asks. There is a pause as the men glance at each other and Walker takes the lead. "Interaction with Nomads does exist. Communication sessions are called 'Exchanges'," Walker explains. He alleges that all Exchanges are handled by a very small, elite Air Force group called Flight Nine. Exchanges may be initiated by either side, but sometimes the Nomads choose not to participate. Exchanges are categorized as Advisory (Nomads to us), Educational, and/or general Question and Answer sessions. Flight Nine's activity is directed by a high level, top secret, Multi Agency Joint Intelligence Committee (MAJIC). "Like the Majestic 12?" Max asks. "No such thing as Majestic 12. There was a Majestic back in the 1950s, but that was a weapons project. Our guess is someone heard the term 'Majestic' and fabricated Majestic 12. We can only guess that the 12 members were conceived based on a jury concept, but the MJ12 documents are unquestionably fakes," responds Raymend.

Walker discloses that the "Batphone" is the code name for a communications device provided by the Nomads and the conventional wisdom is that some foreign governments have these devices too. From 1947 to the late 1960s communications with the Nomads was quite primitive by today's standards. They communicate on a light energy basis that we are just beginning to understand. The Nomads solution was to link with our existing technology. So, initial communication was achieved using old teletypewriters attached to a black cube approximately 6 x 6 x 6 inches provided by BEEs. The box appears solid with no seams and no wires. How it linked to the teletypes is unknown, but given the Nomads technological savvy, not surprising.

Walker explains that scientists were instructed to place the box alongside the teletype and it would pick up the signals as characters were typed, transmitting them in some form to the Nomads; not unlike our current Wi-Fi or cell phone technology. Scientists originally taped the box to the side of the teletype for security using foil duct tape. Late in the 1960s operators started referring to the teletype as the Batphone, no doubt due to the popularity of the Batman TV show. Today we use a specially designed computer system dedicated to Exchanges. Over the years our technology has progressed to where our system converts our speech to text and their text response to speech using computer aided voice synthesizers. Although the Nomads can speak any language, they have insisted on this form of communication. We think it is because of their apparent policy limiting the technology they share and avoiding direct contact. The black box hasn't changed, but subsequent analysis shows it is a solid ceramic of some type with a pyramid-shaped crystal core. The core appears to vibrate when communicating.

Even more fascinating, Walker announces "Marvin" is the code name for the Nomad that communicates with us. Walker maintains, "Marvin has been the only Nomad involved in any Exchange as far as we can tell," and explains there are no large TV screens with an alien face and a give and take discussion like we see in the movies. He clarifies by explaining the Nomads communicate amongst themselves on a consciousness level which is the reason for all the interest in psi during the 1970s and 1980s. It's not telepathy but some means that allows the Nomads to tap into common thoughts, which is well outside our comprehension. So, the Exchanges are all on a textual level more like internet messaging or email and the Batphone is essentially a translation device that converts Nomads communication to a written form that we can understand. "We don't know why they prefer this method," Walker muses out loud. He adds that the Batphone provides bulk information download directly to the computer when needed for large data files and graphical images, for example. Farmer clarifies that the Batphone does not use a radio frequency, but a much higher frequency carrier in the light range. "SETI is looking for the wrong signals," he quips.

Coincidentally, Walker submits that it is not a secret SRI International, a research institute in California, was recently awarded a contract to develop the Broad Operational Language Technology (BOLT) program. The goal of this program is to create technology capable of translating multiple foreign languages in all genres and retrieving information from the translated material as well as enabling bilingual communication via speech or text. The goal is a type of a "universal" translator. Whether or not this has any connection to the Nomads is unclear, but Walker has spoken with some developers who have made some intriguing comments.

Walker indicates that there has never been any official direct, in-person contact with real Nomads or other ETs. Stories of meetings between government officials and Nomads are simply not true; however, there has been contact with BEEs. Leaders have tried to arrange face to face meetings with the Nomads, but their requests have been denied without explanation.

"So, what about the stories of abductions?" Max questions. "Not true. Investigations were conducted into abduction stories to determine if there was a real threat to U.S. citizens," Walker responds definitively. He admits that originally there was some concern, but in an Exchange regarding abductions, Marvin assured us that physical abductions are not part of their mission and are unnecessary. The Nomads possess technology capable of scanning human physiology and consciousness at a distance. No direct contact is required and the process is imperceptible to human cognition. Subsequently, no evidence was found through any government investigation or Exchange to support the abduction claims, which led to the conclusion that abduction stories were/are unfounded. "Nevertheless, such stories remain a lucrative business for some people," is Walker's observation.

For example, Walker reveals that in one of the earliest cases, Betty and Barney Hill, a top secret, special operations team of investigators staked out the highway in the area where the Hills were allegedly abducted. According to the story, in September of 1961, Betty and Barney Hill had visited Niagara Falls, and Montreal, Quebec, Canada, and were on their way back home to Portsmouth, NH on a clear night. At about 10:15 PM, three miles south of the city of Lancaster, Barney reported seeing what appeared to be a bright star, or planet. This star appeared to be moving erratically and eventually approached their vehicle. The Hill's alleged that at one point, they were taken aboard a space ship and examined by a group of "humanoid" creatures. According to Betty, these creatures appeared nearly human, with black hair, dark eyes, prominent noses and bluish lips. She estimated the "men" stood about five feet to five feet four inches tall. Betty subsequently reported the incident to the local air force base in Pease, NH and the story made media headlines.

Following the Hill's reports, it was decided that the special investigators would monitor highway traffic, late at night, looking for people who may have been on the road the same night and time as the Hills. "This is a very common investigative tactic," Raymend comments. Their diligence paid off when investigators stopped a trucker, described as an average man, about five foot eight inches tall with dark wavy, hair. He reported that he observed the Hills in their car, idling in the middle of the road on the night of the alleged incident.

The trucker stated that when he stopped and approached the Hills car, he noticed a man behind the wheel who appeared to be asleep or unconscious. He did not immediately see Betty. When he checked on the Hills, he stated they were apparently drunk and Betty was slumped in the seat leaning against Barney. The trucker reported that he could smell alcohol on Barney's breath and he saw empty liquor bottles in the car. The trucker stated that he, and his partner who had previously remained with the truck, helped Barney and Betty move the car on to a dirt road just off the highway. The trucker also recalled that Betty was complaining about ruining her clothes.

Walker maintains that according to the investigator's still classified report, the trucker never reported the incident or came forward during the official investigation because he wanted to avoid any publicity. He admitted to the special investigation team that, at the time, he was hauling illegal untaxed cigarettes and liquor from Canada to Boston for an underworld organization. He conceded that he would not have stopped except the car was just sitting in the middle of the highway and was a traffic hazard. At the time of the interview, the trucker was wearing the same black leather jacket he reported he was wearing at the time of the incident. Coincidentally, the investigators found that Barney initially reported that one of the aliens was a dark-haired man wearing a black leather jacket.

The trucker agreed to talk only after the investigators assured him that any information he provided would remain confidential and that they were uninterested in his illegal activities. He was also granted immunity from prosecution for any criminal activity he might disclose, for his cooperation. A subsequent interview was conducted with the driver's partner; a man described only as average with dark features and about five feet six inches tall, who confirmed the event. Walker notes that this investigation occurred before the Hill's hypnosis sessions in 1964. And, that under hypnosis Barney recalled seeing lights approaching him on the road according to hypnotist Benjamin Simon, which seemed to corroborate the trucker's story. At the time, Simon speculated that Barney's recall of the UFO encounter was possibly a fantasy inspired by Betty's previous dreams about UFO abductions.

"What I just told you was classified top secret and never released," Walker points out. He also explains that the investigators were ambivalent as to the Hill's motive for this story and with the Hill's subsequent public disclosure because it was determined there was no real national security threat. According to Walker, this report remains classified top secret because of the investigative techniques used and the covert involvement of federal agencies in a local jurisdiction. Walker was told that investigators monitored the story for many years to determine if there was any new evidence that might change the original assessment. Investigators commented they were amused how the actual story was embellished over the years with various self-serving interpretations contrary to all the original reports and evidence, but their original assessment did not change.

Even so, this story remains a staple of the UFO abduction theorists and UFO conference fare.

Walker recalls another infamous incident. He reveals a similar investigation was conducted by a special investigative team regarding the Travis Walton abduction case only because authorities were concerned Walton may have observed a secret Air Force training exercise. This case occurred in November of 1975 in Arizona's Apache-Sitgreaves National Forest.

According to the report, a logging crew of seven men was clearing forest as part of a government contract. As they were leaving for the day they alleged seeing a "luminous object, shaped like a flattened disc" off in the woods. All of the men stated that Travis Walton was "captivated" by the sight, left the truck to get a closer look and was engulfed by a brilliant bluish light. Fearing for their lives they fled the scene. After a heated discussion, some of the men reported they returned to the scene to see if they could help Travis, but they found no trace of the craft, or Travis. Walton reappeared five days later, apparently disoriented and frightened, with hazy memories of aliens and their craft. The workers took a lie detector test and passed the examination, but in regards to seeing *only* a light in the forest, not a space craft. Walton was also subsequently subjected to a number of polygraph and psychological examinations with varying results.

Walker states the secret investigation determined the only thing Walton and the six other men actually observed were bright lights off in the distant forest. The investigators also determined that the men left Walton behind because they were concerned the lights were police vehicles or other authorities on the mountain. The men wanted to avoid any confrontation with the police because they had been drinking and had alcohol and drugs stashed in the truck. The men were concerned that they could be arrested and would lose their jobs. It was later surmised by the investigative team that either Walton's brother or the foreman found Walton later that night and transported him down the mountain and to a friend's house where Walton stayed for several days.

Walker remarks that investigators admitted they found it curious that Walton's first interviews, after his "ordeal," were with the National Inquirer, rather than with the authorities. The National Inquirer was offering $100,000 at the time for the evidence of a real abduction. They also found it curious that despite Walton's statements that he was disoriented and hazy during his ordeal, Walton was able to describe the space craft and a celestial map in surprising detail. Interestingly, Walton did not pass the required tests to validate his claims for the National Inquirer.

Neither Walton nor the local authorities were aware of the top secret investigation because the investigators disguised themselves as tabloid and newspaper reporters, UFO investigators, law enforcement and even doctors and psychologists. The investigators diligently followed up with just about everyone with whom Walton spoke in addition to the six men who were with him. Satisfied Walton had not observed anything of a classified nature and had not been abducted by aliens, the investigators were indifferent to his abduction story and the investigation remains a secret. The investigators also continued to follow this story for a number of years still finding no evidence of abduction.

Even so, as Walker points out, proponents of Walton's story insist all the men passed polygraph tests. However, the truth is that while some tests showed no deception, other tests were inconclusive.

More to the point, the tests confirmed the men observed *only lights in the forest* and not a space craft. The descriptions of disks or space craft were never part of the original reports and were found to be embellishments after the fact. "Alcohol will do that," Walker quips.

Walker asserts that over the years no credible evidence has been found of any abduction and authorities have been assured by an "unidentified but qualified" source that no abductions were ever performed. Both publically available information and classified documents show that investigators have found consistently that all abductions can be explained by ordinary events such as the side effects from medications, drug and alcohol abuse, sleep paralysis (which has long been recognized as a side effect of prescription sleep aids), stress, dehydration, oxygen deprivation as well as a number of other psychological and physiological disorders too numerous to mention. Walker states unequivocally that the U.S. government does not condone nor consent to any abduction of U.S. citizens by any life forms contrary to the stories found in UFO pop-culture.

"Personally, I find it revealing that many abductees often describe the "aliens'" medical procedures in terms of the medical technology of the day," Walker remarks. He points out that this is obviously more apparent with the older reports when one considers our current knowledge of advanced medical technology and procedures. In other words, in most abduction reports we often hear descriptions of invasive and even painful physical examinations that seem contrary to the ETs level of technological advancement.

Such was the case with Betty and Barney Hill. "So, even if we were not aware of the Nomads technological capability to monitor human physiology from a distance, are we to believe that an alien race so advanced to possess the ability for space travel, does not possess non-invasive x-Ray, MRI or even CT scan capability, for example?" Walker argues. The point Walker is trying to make it that it would be reasonable to question if Betty's story was real or a product of her limited imagination given her description of the typically 1960s medical procedures performed on her. Walker adds that the Nomads have the means to wipe clean any experience from the minds of the abductees. Even mankind has that ability today. "I will concede that Nomads ongoing scrutiny of humankind is a viable motive for surveying human subjects, but what's the motive in leaving a partial, even cloudy memory of the event? One might argue, for the very purpose of observing the effects of the experience," Walker concedes, but submits both would be speculation, not conclusive, and inconsistent with the Nomads statements.

All men agree that there have been, and will continue to be other genuine "UFO" events, but most are misidentifications. "The Nomads can enter and leave our airspace without detection," Tucker interjects and adds, "They have mastered the techniques for complete invisibility, ultimate stealth; a quantum leap beyond Northup-Grumman's electronic invisibility systems." He points out that, it should be noted most genuine civilian UFO incidents and sightings are extremely rare and, were and are, due to malfunctions of the alien technology. It was not supposed to happen. Apparently, even an advanced race must suffer the frustration of technological glitches and failures reports Farmer. Sometimes, it is just a failure of the stealth technology; ET spacecraft carry no navigational lights so what is observed are sensors or propulsion systems. Other times, the failures are catastrophic and the equipment crashes or disintegrates. This is why Projects like Moondust and Blue Fly, or more current and top secret, recovery projects were initiated. In that regard, Walker comments that he has heard of a project called Dustbuster to recover such material.

MANAGING THE THREAT

The five men are unanimous in pointing out that there never has been, and does not appear to be, an immediate threat from the ET visitors. No U.S. aircraft or materiel has ever been intentionally destroyed by Nomads and there is no official record of any aggressive acts towards humankind. However, it is true that some aircraft were damaged or destroyed due to pilot error while exceeding their aircraft's flight capabilities in pursuit of Nomads. Any other incident was the result of crashed or malfunctioning ET technology and not an intentional hostile act. At the same time, the men also agree, that even under such benign circumstances one must remain vigilant that such a relationship does not turn malevolent. Programs aimed at developing weapons to protect against an ET threat have been ongoing since the early 1960s. And, the men concede it is true that some of the largest black-budget projects fund the construction of top secret subterranean command, control and survival centers as a safeguard against a potential threat.

According to Raymend, what is unknown to most Americans is that a major portion of the so-called black budget is used to manage the ET threat and gather EXINTEL. Hartman concurs with a nod as he cleans his glasses. EXINTEL or extraterrestrial intelligence is any information concerning Nomads and any other ET entity. Allegedly, NASA, DARPA and NASIC are major players in support of these operations. "Anyone but me notice that the NASA emblem has a saucer shaped craft at leading edge of the elliptical vapor trail encircling the NASA logo?" interjects Tucker. Walker's eyes narrow as he thinks about the logo for a moment and then nods in affirmation. EXINTEL is classified Top Secret and compartmented under the control, FIREFLY.

Raymend continues. He contends that small, top secret elements of the USAF Space Command, NASIC, NASA and the lesser known NRO (National Reconnaissance Office) work with the USAF to monitor potential ET threats. The NRO is the U.S. Government agency in charge of designing, building, launching, and maintaining America's intelligence satellites. But even though these groups may work together, certain information is compartmented to minimize security risks and limit personnel's awareness of the scope of the ET situation. Even so, all personnel are bound by an oath of secrecy and the penalties for violating that oath can be severe. Accordingly, various objectives are assigned to different units or sections.

Each section has access to resources from their counterparts in other intelligence and military organizations. For example, the intelligence section monitors all forms of ET activity and conducts espionage to acquire any information held by foreign governments. This includes monitoring and manipulating the public flow of UFO-related data in all forms of media, as well as disinformation programs and the recovery of classified documents or evidence that may have fallen into public domain. To accomplish this, the intelligence unit may employ electronic surveillance and data collection through the NSA (National Security Agency). The NSA is a U.S. government intelligence organization responsible for global monitoring, collection, and processing of information and data for intelligence and counterintelligence purposes through active and passive electronic means. The engineering section reverse engineers all forms of ET technology and documents that knowledge for our own technological development. This section can draw upon the resources of the military addition to defense contractors through carve-out projects. Flight Nine manages Exchange communications. Agents of these groups may be working undercover in just about any organization, public or private.

The concern over UFO secrets leaking into the public sector is taken seriously, but has become less acute. According to Raymend, the intelligence community recognizes that the UFO pop-culture has flooded the media with so much misinformation, exaggeration and pure fiction, based often on pseudo-science and superficial research, that much of the work of maintaining secrecy and planting disinformation has been done. As a result, the opinion is just about any information, unless released by the highest levels of government authority, will always be considered dubious by the public. And then, growing distrust of the government will lead many people to question official announcements as well. Tucker points out that, because of this information "clutter", it has become unnecessary to completely control the flow of data because once mixed with the clutter, the truth has become indistinguishable from the fantasy.

Still, the government believes it is important to keep track of any viable UFO-related information that ends up in the public domain. This means it is necessary to recover any physical evidence or documents that could provide corroboration for the UFO hypothesis. In other words, the government is somewhat ambivalent as to what information is disclosed or leaked to the public as long as there is no evidence to support it. Unbeknownst to the UFO community, members of these intelligence groups have connections in just about every UFO organization regardless of their size or notoriety.

Tucker concedes somewhat contritely that there is little understood about Nomads technology except for its capabilities. Access to the Roswell crystals has been problematic. The concept of storing data on a light-wave or frequency basis is just beginning to be understood. Tucker believes that unlocking the secrets of data storage in the Roswell crystals could yield an incredible volume of information, not to mention that some ancient crystal artifacts might also be data storage mediums given to early civilizations long ago by ET visitors.

Using light energy to store data is not necessarily a new concept. Holographic data storage is possible and provides great potential in the field of high-capacity data storage according to IBM. Tucker explains that data storage is currently limited to magnetic data storage and conventional optical data storage. Magnetic and optical data storage devices rely on individual bits (8 bits equal a byte and one byte equals one character) being stored as distinct magnetic or optical conditions on the surface of the recording medium using a binary format (0's or 1's). Alternatively, holographic data storage records information by utilizing light at different angles. Whereas magnetic and optical data storage records information one bit at a time in a linear fashion, holographic storage is capable of recording and reading millions of bits concurrently. This allows data transfer and storage rates much greater than those available with traditional storage media. Tucker adds that IBM was successful at building a memory chip that uses light energy to store data, but found that creating an interface using current computing technology is problematic.

Tucker goes on to reveal with some concern that Nomads have demonstrated an unrestricted access to our electronic information grid. And, such unrestricted electronic data and communications access may currently be the biggest threat to our civilization. According to Walker, one of the most astounding discoveries was that the Nomads don't necessarily need technology to tap into our electronic information transmissions. Apparently, their minds can process and decode transmissions directly, just like we listen to a radio. And the Nomads have developed technology that links with their consciousness to scan millions of transmissions automatically and provide a kind of an "index" for any particular topics in which they may be interested. So, the sobering truth is that there can be no secrets from the Nomads, and they can manipulate data on a global scale whenever they choose.

"This means the Nomads can influence government policy and the course of history by altering data. They can also alter communications between parties and even on a battlefield between forces thus influencing the outcome and we believe they have done so," Tucker declares. He acknowledges that this is partially due to our reliance on the use of satellite-based data transmission which provides an uninterrupted flow of data through the atmosphere. What this means to the average person is we know that the Nomads can, for example, access health information, bank records, monitor phone conversations and even alter that data. "To what end, we're not sure," Tucker concedes.

Walker admits, "What we've learned from HAARP-." "The High-frequency Active Auroral Research Program," Farner interjects. Walker clears his throat and continues, "is that the Nomads do have the ability to read our minds and control behavior using technology."

Walker explains. HAARP was an academic project in the 1990s with the goal of manipulating the ionosphere to improve worldwide communications through the use of electromagnetic radiation. However, Walker points out, that according to the U.S. Air Force, the potential applications of artificial electromagnetic fields can be used in many military or quasi-military situations to control human behavior. The EM (electromagnetic) systems can be used to produce mild to severe physiological disruption and perceptual distortion, or disorientation, in individuals or groups, often described as "Mind Control". This means that the ability for independent thought can be degraded to such a point that individuals are functionally ineffective, Walker clarifies. Another advantage of the electromagnetic methods is that they can provide coverage over large areas, even hemispheres, with a single system. Samantha's eyes are fixed on Walker in fascination and she cups her chin in her hand.

Walker reports that it was determined the Nomads psi or psychic ability is indefensible. They can use their minds to control small groups of people in close proximity simply with their psi ability. EMF technology is likely used on a broad scale when a global effect is desired. And, there is concern that some of this knowledge may have fallen into the hands of foreign governments. Again, this technology is all based on the Nomads mastery of electromagnetic forces.

Walker notes that around 1976, Dr. Sam Koslov, the scientific assistant to the secretary of the U.S. Navy, became aware of various contracts held by the Navy, including one with SRI described as "ELF AND MIND CONTROL" (ELF stands for Extremely-Low Frequency). It was reported that Koslov cancelled the contract with SRI for ethical reasons; however, unknown to Koslov, the project moved forward using funds from the black budget with the objective of learning the extent of the ET technology's capability and using ELFs to possibly counter the Nomads advantage. Walker also points out it was quickly recognized that the use of ELFs had possible political applications, and as a result, some of the knowledge gained was applied in domestic and international covert operations designed to advance the CIA's geopolitical influence, and by foreign governments during the Vietnam War for political subversion.

Walker also concedes that in the 1980s the Soviets had a decided advantage in EMF and ELF research. This concerned President Reagan for many reasons. At the very least, it was determined that EMF and ELF could affect human cognition in addition to providing a new communications medium and the potential for advanced weaponry. More importantly, it was believed EMF technology provided the opportunity for greatly enhanced communications with the Nomads as well as a planetary early warning system, and new technology that might offer a defensive capability against ETs.

Reagan also knew that the Nomads ongoing surveillance of earth was a disturbing fact. Nomads' satellites were hidden in space junk orbiting the Earth and possessed more than just the capability for surveillance. Farmer claims it was discovered that some of the domestic power outages that occurred over the years, such as the Great Eastern States Blackout of 1965, was precipitated by the Nomads technology, which is effective against mechanical as well electronic equipment. Raymend is quick to concede it is also true that in some other cases our own classified research on weapons for disrupting power grids were to blame for outages. "Like carbon fiber?" Farmer muses. Raymend concurs with a nod and a sly smile.

If Max and Samantha were not already feeling a little anxious, Farmer has a more disturbing revelation. There is evidence that the Nomads have the ability to manipulate natural events such as weather and geophysical activity as well as asteroids, meteors, solar events, and even redirect forms of cosmic radiation such as gamma rays arising from astronomical activity. "Is that solar flare natural or incited by some advanced technology?" Farmer questions rhetorically, but his tone suggests he already knows the answer. In other words, their technology provides the Nomads the ability to manipulate radiation from the sun and other celestial bodies. According to Walker, NASA, NASIC and the USAF Space Command have groups focused on addressing such capabilities, which led to the HARRP project, and with which Farmer is quite familiar. He worked on the project for DARPA.

Every conspiracy theorist will be quick to assert that the real purpose of HAARP, at the very least, was weather modification by manipulating the upper atmosphere using a burst of charged particles. These particles cause modifications of the atmosphere on a molecular level resulting in changes to weather patterns. In fact, Bernard J. Eastlund's U.S. Patent # 4,686,605, "Method and Apparatus for Altering a Region in the Earth's Atmosphere, Ionosphere; and/or Magnetosphere," clearly describes how such weather modification is possible. "Some people felt this was ground-breaking, but attempts at weather manipulation were not new," Farmer confesses.

Farmer explains that the U.S. Department of Defense conducted studies aimed at lightning and hurricane manipulation in Project Skyfire and Project Stormfury during the 1950's and 1960's. The military also studied both lasers and chemical means to damage the ozone layer over enemy forces and territory. A project called Prime Argus studied ways to cause earthquakes, as well as to detect them, decades ago. The funding for all these projects came from

DARPA. Farmer contends that the upside for the government was that all this activity was prime fodder for the conspiracy theorists, successfully deflecting their attention from the real ET-related objectives, and disinformation programs became less crucial.

Farmer continues by pointing out that during the 1960's attempts were also made to better track any foreign activity over U.S. airspace. However, the term "foreign" was expanded to include extraterrestrial as well as terrestrial threats, but this was not publicized in the non-classified public project disclosures. The ET situation was becoming more of a concern. To this end, the Air Force created the Air Force Space Surveillance System (AFSSS) also known as the "Fence" described publicly as an early warning system against enemy missile attacks, but that was just part of the mission. The "Fence" transmitter array and receivers create a continent-wide energy field in space much like an electronic blanket covering the United States. Satellites or other objects passing through the energy field or "Fence" can be easily detected. The "Fence" mission is to maintain a constant surveillance of space and identify any objects entering U.S. air space.

Farmer explains that there are nine "FENCE" arrays located on a path across the southern United States from Georgia to California along the 33rd parallel. These arrays include three transmission and six receiver sites. The transmission, or illumination, sites broadcast a signal into the atmosphere and the receiver sites monitor the signals reflection off any objects in that space. The main broadcasting station is located at Lake Kickapoo, Texas, and has an average power output of almost 800,000 watts that provides the power for a two-mile long antenna array. The Lake Kickapoo station provides the primary broadcast, or illumination, source. Two other broadcasting stations are located at Jordan Lake, Alabama, and Gila River,

Arizona. These stations, which have an average power output of approximately 40,000 watts each, provide low altitude illumination at the sides of the main beam in effect creating a dome effect to the blanket, Farmer lectures.

The receiving stations are located across the United States at Tattnall, Georgia; Hawkinsville, Georgia; Silver Lake, Mississippi; Red River, Arkansas; Elephant Butte, New Mexico; and San Diego, California. The stations at Hawkinsville and Elephant Butte have larger antenna arrays enabling high altitude detection in addition to low earth capability. Energy emitted from the broadcast sites form a fixed, fan shaped beam in the north-south direction extending across the continental United States in the east-west direction. This ensures that one or more of the receiver sites will detect energy reflected from objects penetrating the beam. "Nevertheless," Farmer adds, "even given a continental tracking capacity, the aspiration was still to create, a global, object tracking capability."

Aside from the tracking and surveillance initiatives, Raymend states that in the late 1970s, as more was being learned about the Nomads, it was determined that action must be taken to create some type of defensive capability against potential ET threats. At the time, new technology was becoming available that could theoretically provide effective weapons systems. According to Raymend, an initiative called the Solar Powered Satellite (SPS) project was considered. As early as 1968 the U.S. military had proposed Solar Powered Satellites be placed in geostationary orbit, approximately 22,000 miles above the earth. The political selling-point was these satellites could accumulate solar radiation using solar cells and transmit the energy via a microwave beam to receiving antennas on earth, called rectennas. About ten years later, the U.S. Congress instructed the Department of

Energy and NASA to prepare an Environmental Impact Assessment on this project. The impact assessment was completed in June 1980. It was estimated the project would cost $25 million.

Raymend points out the real secret was that although SPS was originally conceived as a solar energy program, it was recognized in the late 1970's that SPS actually had significant military implications to meet a more urgent need. More specifically, one was the possibility for developing a satellite-borne beam weapon for anti-ballistic missile (ABM) use. "More importantly, was the hope that it could provide some level of protection against Nomads should they become hostile," is Farmer's assertion, and he points out that neither of these objectives were disclosed publically and the ET ramifications were known only to a very few. "And, as long as the program was called 'solar energy', it could not be considered a 'weapons' project in violation of any space treaties," Raymend remarks.

Farmer explains the concept called for SPS satellites to be located in geosynchronous orbits with each providing a vantage point from which an entire hemisphere could be continuously surveyed. It was speculated, at the classified level, that a high-energy laser beam could function as a thermal weapon to disable or destroy enemy threats. There was also some discussion of an electron beam weapon which would follow a pre-heated path through the atmosphere created by a laser beam. Interestingly, SPS was also capable of causing physical changes in the ionosphere; shades of HAARP. Farmer claims, "While on the surface SPS was described as an anti-ballistic missile shield, its dual objective was to provide a planetary defense system against Nomads."

Then President Carter approved the SPS project and gave it a go-ahead in spite of the reservations expressed by some of his advisors, who were unaware of the more furtive ET objectives. Farmer points out that, "Carter was not actually aware of the real urgency in regard to Nomads, but supported the project on the grounds of an anti-ballistic missile defense." Unfortunately, it was considered too expensive; funding was denied by the Congress because they too were unaware of the real ET threat. And, at the time, the ET threat was considered less significant than would be the impact of disclosing the existence of the Nomads. Farmer notes, "Interestingly, the same project resurfaced under President Reagan. He moved it to the much larger Department of Defense budget and called it 'Star Wars.'" Reagan, on the other hand, was aware of the Nomads threat. "Many people thought the "Star Wars' reference was used simply because of the popularity of the movie, but its implications were much more serious than anyone realized," Raymend remarks.

"The conspiracy theorists accusations of weather modification and possible cognitive effects from HAARP are not incorrect, but the real purpose has been locked in secrecy," is Walker's contention. HAARP projects were an attempt to discover the Nomads secret to mastering electromagnetic fields and EM radiation. From Farmer's perspective, HAARP's real objectives were ambitious to say the least, and as it turns out, quite dangerous. Simply put, HAARP's priorities were to learn to master EMFs and radiation with the goals of creating an early warning system against ETs in addition to developing an advanced defensive EMF "force" field and beam weapon. At the same time, researchers were hypothesizing on the ability to disturb EMFs in the atmosphere as a means to interfere with Nomads propulsion systems as well as block their use of EMF technology for surveillance purposes. The Cold war applications were a bonus. "Unfortunately, the original HAARP project was a dangerous flirtation with science beyond our understanding, which ultimately damaged the environment, even though it did provide some technological advancement," Farmer confesses.

The lecture continues with each man contributing his unique piece of the puzzle. Max periodically gets up and paces as he tries to wrap his mind around what he is hearing. Hartman cleans his glasses even though one would suspect they should be clean by now. Farmer concedes HAARP yielded important discoveries regarding communications, object detection and weapon systems as potential tools against the Nomads. It also provided a means to disable conventional enemy communication systems over an extremely large area, while allowing the U.S. military's own communications systems to function uninterrupted. Farmer also notes that HAARP technology could be used to replace over-the-horizon radar systems with a more flexible and accurate system that would be beneficial against contemporary enemies as well as Nomads.

"The fact is, HAARP made existing technologies obsolete," Farmer states. It was also determined that the technology could confuse or completely disrupt airplanes' and missiles' sophisticated guidance systems and it was hoped this would be effective against ET threats. Perhaps most importantly, the tool provided the ability to create pulsed-beam weapons by focusing unprecedented amounts of power in the Earth's atmosphere at strategic locations. The resulting effect simulated the detonation of nuclear devices of various yields at different altitudes. "This means the military had a tool to replace the electromagnetic pulse effect of atmospheric thermonuclear devices," Farmer explains and adds that the same technology has the ability to modify large regions of the atmosphere so that missiles and other "aircraft" encounter unexpected drag forces that result in instability and ultimately, destruction of the craft. "Despite the downsides,

HAARP technology was considered essential for national security and as the only viable defense against an ET threat," he argues.

"The Nomads bag of tricks seems endless," Farmer quips as he discloses that Nomads stealth is absolute. It is not just the radar evading capability with which we have become familiar, but rather actual "cloaking" or true invisibility; a quantum leap more advanced than Northrop's electronic invisibility programs. He reveals it was determined that most Nomads craft are auto-piloted drones or piloted by the BEEs. Actual aliens or Nomads enter the atmosphere only under special circumstances. "As we mentioned before, many UFO incidents and sightings were and are a result of malfunctions of the alien technology, be it the aircraft, avionics or even the BEEs," Farmer reminds the group. According to Farmer, most actual sightings were not supposed to happen. And, these "failures" compromise the stealth capabilities, where once again, the HAARP project may have provided some assistance. HAARP provided technology to better monitor the geomagnetic flux, a donut-shaped band of magnetic energy around the earth, to sense ET activity. This is analogous to the workings of a spider web. The HAARP technology can detect vibrations in the Earth's electromagnetic fields similar to when an insect lands on a spider web and the web's vibrations alert the spider to possible prey. "But all this came at a cost," Farmer laments with the shake of his head in an uncharacteristic display of emotion.

"It was discovered that HAARPs electromagnetic energy bursts had a profound effect on the migration patterns of fish and wild animals which rely on an undisturbed energy field to find their routes," Farmer reveals. He also maintains that the resulting unnatural level of highly-energized particles in the atmosphere and in radiation belts surrounding Earth is believed to be the underlying factor in recent weather disruptions as well as the planet attempting to discharge its buildup of heat, relieve stress and regain a balanced ecosystem through earthquakes and volcanic action.

"Nevertheless, we are now in the process of developing new and more effective EMF/energy-based technology," Farmer asserts. He explains that Lockheed Martin for example, is developing technology for a new Space Fence that will enhance the way the U.S. Air Force identifies and tracks objects in space. According to the press releases, "Space Fence" as it is called, will use new ground and space-based radars to provide the Air Force with automatic detection, tracking and accurate measurement of space objects. The geographic separation of tracking stations and the higher frequency of the new Space Fence radars will allow for the detection of much smaller microsatellites and debris than the current technology. Additionally, the new Space Fence design will significantly improve the timeliness with which operators can detect space events that could present potential threats to GPS satellites or the International Space Station.

Space Fence will replace the existing Air Force Space Surveillance System, or Fence, which has been in service since the early 1960s. The new system is scheduled to go online in 2017. But, Farmer is quick to point out "The real secret is this new system will provide a distinct advantage against conventional - as well as - ET related threats. But that little piece of information has been omitted from the public disclosures."

Farmer confesses that he has worked on high-altitude, space-based weapons employing EM technology. He maintains that it has been proven that these weapons can destroy and disrupt electronic and electrical devices by causing a burst of electromagnetic radiation (electromagnetic pulse, or EMP). Farmer explains that these bursts are commonly associated with nuclear explosions; however, scientists have produced non-nuclear EMP's that mimic Nomad technology, but not nearly as powerful. Nevertheless, these small EM bursts pose a significant threat to aircraft by scrambling their avionics if not "hardened" against the effect. "Is this what the lightning strike did at Roswell?" Raymend muses coyly as if offering a hint.

"EMF research has contributed to the development of particle beam weapons, also known as directed-energy weapons (DEW), not unlike the phasers in Star Trek," Farmer asserts. Samantha and Max sit in rapt silence. Is this guy for real they wonder as Farmer states his case? It is a scientific fact that current particle beam weapons generate power many times more destructive than any laser in development. The features that make DEW so attractive include their ability to fire their "bolts" at or near the speed of light (186,000 miles a second), which would effectively freeze even high-speed targets in motion, as well as their ability to redirect their fire toward multiple targets very rapidly. In addition, is their extreme long range as in thousands of miles in space, and their ability to transmit lethal doses of energy in seconds or even fractions of a second. Plus, no conventional dangerously volatile and heavy ammunition is necessary; only fuel for the power generator is required.

Farmer explains the "bolts" of energy fired from the particle beam weapon are absorbed by the target's structural materials and result in a rapid increase in the material's temperature. This excites the molecules causing the object to explode in only a matter of seconds after impact of the beam. The characteristic that distinguishes the particle-beam weapon from other directed energy weapons is the form of energy it employs. While there are several operating concepts for particle-beam weapons, all such devices generate their destructive power by accelerating subatomic particles or atoms to velocities near the speed of light and focusing these particles into a very high-energy beam. Currently, the particles being used to form the beam are electrons, protons, or hydrogen atoms.

Farmer points to evidence that reveals the U.S. has already tested EM beam weapons. The Sandia National Laboratory built a 250,000 square foot laboratory on the Kirtland Air Force Base back in 1989 to house the Hermes II electron beam generator. Hermes II produced 20 trillion watt pulses that lasted, at the time, 20-to-25 billionths-of-a-second. The Hermes II simulator was called a "Particle Beam Fusion Accelerator". Similar experiments revealed a stream of electrons hitting a metal plate can produce a pulsed X-ray or gamma ray. Farmer admits there is no consensus for a definition distinguishing between X-rays and gamma rays. But, one common practice is to distinguish between the two types of radiation based on their source: X-rays are emitted by electrons, while gamma rays are emitted by the atomic nucleus. One other common alternative is to distinguish X and gamma radiation on the basis of wavelength or frequency. He notes that hot gases in the Universe emit X-rays and the Universe is the biggest gamma-ray generator of all. "And, apparently energy the Nomads have harnessed," Famer concedes.

According to Farmer, more sophisticated EM devices were tested during the Gulf War. One such event was reported in the April 13-19, 1992 edition of the "Defense News," which revealed that the U.S. deployed an electromagnetic pulse weapon (EMP) during Desert Storm, designed to mimic the flash of electricity from a nuclear bomb. Farmer explains that other types of directed-energy weapons utilize lasers, high-powered microwaves, and the particle beams that he described previously. The U.S. has a number of successful ongoing projects including the Airborne Laser, the Active Denial System, and the Tactical High Energy Laser (THEL). "And I'm sure there are projects that we're not aware of that are even more fantastic," Raymend remarks.

"One of the most highly classified space weapons in development is the U.S. Air Force's space plane, the X-37B," Farmer reveals, but admits that designation may no longer be applicable. "Most of the details about X-37 flights are classified and it reportedly has links with the flying triangles," he explains. Farmer also concedes that the plane is not the only secret flying object the U.S. government is operating in space, but he is not willing to go into details. "There are hundreds of military satellites and vehicles orbiting in space. The secret space programs are as large as the public NASA programs. To what end?" he taunts them.

A number of other top secret projects are underway to support the objectives of ET defense, Raymend informs them, such as the Electromagnetic Pulsed Field Array (EMPULSE) also known as Project Glow Worm. This is analogous to an electronic spider web cast over the planet which has the power to detect as well as destroy targets globally. During testing it sometimes causes a glow in the sky similar to the Aurora Borealis, hence the nickname Glow Worm. And, the Electromagnetic Field Dampering System or Project Sky Bubble, which is believed to be a means to create an anti-gravitational field, or bubble, surrounding objects such as an aircraft. This anti-gravitational field can then be manipulated to take advantage of the fluctuations in earth's magnetic field to push or pull aircraft through the atmosphere. "All this has been aided by Exchanges with the Nomads even though they are careful not to reveal anything other than concepts and principles," notes Raymend. "This research is no doubt the source of some current UFO reports," Farmer suggests.

"We are also trying to determine from where exactly the Nomads come," Raymend reveals. In addition to military initiatives, he claims this aspect of threat management is woven into the U.S. public space exploration programs although this is unknown to most of the civilian project teams. One highly classified objective of current space probes, like Cassini, Dawn, Mariner and Voyager, is to discover the Nomads hiding places within our solar system. Again, unbeknownst to the civilian project teams, a top secret group of analysts scours every piece of information generated by each mission looking for ET signatures throughout the solar system. It was also recognized that orbiting satellites would provide greater surveillance capability for tracking Nomads in addition to their more terrestrial missions, so in some cases have dual missions. There are a number of otherwise innocuous satellites with secret sensing instruments onboard. Raymend is quick to comment that the space program was initially a lightning rod aimed at attracting more substantial contact with the Nomads. According to Raymend, it was believed the Nomads had a base on the moon.

There is a rare moment of silence as Walker rises and pours himself another cup of hot chocolate. Max and Samantha sit motionless just glancing around the room and at the participants as if trying to internalize what they are hearing. Max stands, take a deep breath and goes over to a window. What he sees outside is a very familiar scene and it offers him a sense of normalcy. Max turns back into the room and that feeling is quickly replaced by a sense of anything but normal. The men are talking amongst themselves. Samantha is speaking with Shepherd. Max sits back down next to Samantha.

Shepherd stares into Max's eyes and arches his brow as if saying, "I warned you!"

Samantha takes Max's hand as the men turn their attention back to the discussion. There seems to be some confusion as to who will speak next, but Tucker steps up after a series of glances between the men. "Who is your neighbor?" he asks. Max and Samantha are unsure how to respond. Tucker sees the blank expression on their faces and explains. As mentioned before it is unknown just how many Nomads actually visit earth, however they have indicated that they do so. Tucker alleges that according to the photo images provided by the Nomads, they look incredibly similar to us contrary to all the sci-fi depictions and the stories from UFO reports. They tend to be tall and fair skinned, not short and grey. Those are the BEEs. However, it is acknowledged that there are specially trained Nomads along with a "population" of what are called Biologically Engineered Human Facsimiles, referred to as MUTTS, who are long term residents on Earth. We do not know the numbers of this population, but they are virtually indistinguishable from humans and almost impossible to track down. Walker chuckles to himself. The others look at him hoping for an explanation. Walker notices their gaze and smiles. "Marvin once made reference to the happiest place on Earth. I guess he went on vacation," Walker chortles in a rare display of nerdy humor.

Only two MUTTS have been discovered by accident. "Quite literally, in 1978 two were involved in a motor vehicle accident near the Lockheed Skunk Works," Tucker quips. He explains that while their physiology is similar to humans, it was different enough to arouse suspicion in one of the treating physicians, a former Air Force flight surgeon who had been involved in top secret projects.

The physician reported the situation to a military contact and the bodies were removed under, what seemed to the other members of the medical staff, suspicious circumstances. The medical staff was directed by intelligence personnel not to discuss the incident with anyone, citing medical privacy restrictions and some esoteric story about the victims being involved in espionage or such. As a side note, Raymend states that although we have been told that actual Nomads are resident on Earth, none have ever been discovered. "We suspect in such cases they handle any personal medical-type issues directly," is Tucker's explanation.

This is a lot to swallow even for Samantha. She shakes her head in a mix of confusion and skepticism. "Why haven't the Tutoribus come for you?" Samantha inquires provocatively. "We believe they know we share a doomsday pact. If anything suspicious should happen to any one of us, the others will publically reveal what they know," is Hartman answer. "This meeting may have changed that," Raymend adds ominously. He exchanges glances with the others and they seem to already know that their immunity has been compromised. "Surely you are not the only ones who know about this," Samantha remarks. "There is only a handful. But, we have broken the rules by speaking with you. We understand the risks and it is our choice," is Raymend's response.

Raymend explains that the Tutoribus seem to stay away from government personnel apparently knowing they are bound by their oath of secrecy. That can change if the personnel break that confidence. "Most people know nothing of the Tutoribus until it's too late," Farmer remarks. Even so, Raymend contends that many people report being visited by men alleging to be from the government following their departure from government service. These men remind them of their oath of secrecy and the severe penalties for violating that oath. "We were all visited. And we know the men were not from the government," Tucker comments. Attempt to determine their identities are futile. "The dark side is that there have been 'accidents' and we lost some people who, coincidentally, revealed ET information; people who had actual evidence to back up their claims. Needless to say, the evidence disappeared following their deaths," Raymend laments.

If this is scam, Max is going to play along. It's all too fantastic to be true and, again, regardless of Raymend's explanation, why tell me, he wonders? Max is also suspicious of Shepherd. He is hiding something. Max provokes the men, "So, let's say I buy all this. Is there a threat to humanity or not?" "Your petulance is not conducive to this discussion, Mr. Park," Shepherd chastises him. "I apologize. That was not my intention, but you have to admit I have cause to be skeptical," Max replies contritely. "Agreed," booms Raymend. "There is no immediate threat of invasion and any concern over ET craft posing some type of aeronautical navigational hazard is unwarranted," is Farmer's contention. Max gets up and shakes his head as he paces, unsure of how to deal with these impossible revelations. "We understand this is hard to believe," Raymend concedes. "You don't know us and we have no physical evidence to prove our story, but I have neither the time nor inclination to play games," he adds. And Raymend is the type of man that when he speaks, you believe him.

GLOBAL DOMINANCE AND THE ET ADVANTAGE

Surely this is a dream and Max figures he will wake up at any moment. It's just too bizarre. Are these people delusional or just outright crazy? Everything he has been taught tells Max this is impossible. What does he really know about Samantha and Shepherd? But what possible motive could they have to lie? And after all, he contacted Samantha. She didn't come looking for him. If all this is true, Max can understand why no one ever talks about it; no one would believe it. But the stakes are about to get higher.

Hartman has listened patiently to the others, but now he has another agenda on his mind. He takes off his glasses and cleans then again. Hartman slips his glasses back on and clears his throat to attract everyone's attention. "The Nomads are only half of the equation. The immediate danger is not from some extraterrestrial invasion, but the age old quest for world domination," he announces. Hartman is not talking about some esoteric amalgam of business and government conjured up by the conspiracy theorists, but rather players like the U.S., U.K., Russia and China. Hartman speaks of classified top secret documents that refer to global dominance euphemistically as "world security". This is the philosophy of a group of people who believe that world peace can be achieved only through world dominance. And, they also believe possession of ET technology is the key to achieve that goal. Among U.S. intelligence analysts there is a concern that other governments have access to ET technology that may discover its secrets before the U.S. and use the technology to their advantage. Any group that possesses and understands how to use such advanced technology could change the balance of world power and threaten world domination.

Hartman claims that this quest for ET technology has resulted in a super-secret field of espionage known only to an elite few. Most presidents, heads of state and legislators know nothing of this shadowy world on the fringe of reality. The goal is to acquire the Nomads technology and prevent others from possessing it. The latter of which appears to be the sole objective of the Tutoribus. The prize is a weapons platform that will compel worldwide acquiescence. Hartman believes that for decades, the petty squabbles of the Cold War diverted attention from this real battle to dominate space and control the world.

Hartman pauses for a moment as if there is something he wants to say, but not sure if he should say it. "There was a rumor," he starts. "There was a rumor in the late 1970s that some brief discussions considered the idea that the U.S. and Soviet Union could use their combined might to share control of the world and provide a united front against the Nomads. The U.N. was considered to be impotent. But, allegedly the U.S. and Soviets couldn't decide on the territorial division of the planet or a common ideology with which they would govern," Hartman reveals. Raymend does not seem surprised by Hartman's allegation, but the expressions on their faces indicate the others are clearly shocked by this revelation. "I doubt neither was ready to give up their secrets," Hartman adds as an afterthought.

Hartman explains the Nomads have shown little interest in world affairs, but apparently do not want to see any of their technology serve as a means for global dominance. That is why, when the Nomads lose a piece of technology, they come looking for it. It is believed that some of the UFO incidents reported at certain military installations are the Nomads returning to reclaim their property. "So, where is all this stuff hidden, Area 51?" Max inquires. "Wouldn't that be a little obvious; to keep it in a place where everyone is looking?" Raymend scoffs. Max thinks about it for a moment and then nods contritely in concession.

Area 51 is a secret U.S. Air Force facility located within the Nevada Test and Training Range just adjacent to Nellis AFB in Southern Nevada. The "Area 51" designation refers to a specific sector on the range. The actual names for the facility are Homey Airport and Groom Lake, although the name Area 51 was found in a CIA document dating from the Vietnam War. Other names have been used for the facility, which include Dreamland, and the nicknames Paradise Ranch, Home Base and Watertown. The airspace surrounding the facility is for special use only and highly restricted without specific authorization. That includes military as well as civilian aircraft. The base's primary purpose is to support the development and testing of experimental aircraft and weapons systems which are referred to as black projects, but is also the main facility for the reverse-engineering of foreign aircraft such as the Russian MIG, for example.

The intense secrecy surrounding the base makes it the frequent subject of conspiracy theories and a central component in UFO folklore. In that regard, many in the UFO culture believe the remains of crashed alien technology is located at Area 51. The base has never been officially declared a secret base, but all research and activity in Area 51 is classified top secret. A FOIA request was filed in

2005 concerning Area 51. But, it was not until 2013 that the U.S. government publicly acknowledged the existence of the base for the first time, and also declassified selected documents detailing the history and mission of Area 51. Interestingly, no information was released regarding a facility referred to as Area S4 just south of Area 51.

According to Raymend, pieces of the Roswell debris went to Wright-Patterson and no doubt to the old Griffis Air Force Base in Rome, New York. "But, it's not at Area 51 or some remote secret base in the mountains of Utah. All I can tell you is that it's in a building that looks like a typical corporate office, in a typical corporate office park, and away from the prying eyes of spy satellites. People drive by it every day and don't know it. This is a place where even some of the employees are unaware of the material's presence," Raymend boasts.

Max sits down next to Samantha. Just when he was thinking this could not get any stranger, it does. He glances at Samantha. He can tell by the incredulous look on Samantha's face that if this is a scam, she knows nothing about it. This all sounds like one of those bad, black and white sci-fi movies from the 1950s. Every instinct Max has tells him it is time to grab Samantha and leave, but something makes him want to hear more. Incredibly, this is actually starting to make sense, he thinks.

"Would you like to know more?" Hartman asks. Samantha encourages Max with a subtle nod. "What does all this have to do with Roswell," Max replies. "The contents of the Roswell craft hold the secret to technology that can assure global dominance. Colonel Philip Corso was telling the truth," Farmer testifies. Philip James Corso served in the United States Army from February 1942 to March 1963, and rose to the rank of Lieutenant Colonel. In 1997, Corso published *The Day After Roswell*, a book detailing how he was involved in the research of extraterrestrial technology recovered from the 1947 Roswell UFO Incident.

In his book, Corso claims he was responsible for reverse-engineering extraterrestrial technology recovered from the Roswell crash. It was Corso's allegation that a top secret government group was assembled under the leadership of the first Director of Central Intelligence, Adm. Roscoe H. Hillenkoetter to secure all information regarding "off-planet" technology. This was ongoing while the U.S. government was simultaneously publicly discounting the existence of "flying saucers". According to Corso, reverse engineering of the Roswell technology indirectly led to the development of accelerated particle beam devices, fiber optics, lasers, integrated circuit chips and Kevlar material. In the book, Corso also claims the Strategic Defense Initiative (SDI), or "Star Wars", was intended to disable the electronic guidance systems in incoming enemy warheads, as well as disabling enemy spacecraft, including those of *extraterrestrial origin*. "This is where your triangles come in kid," Tucker quips, but this time Farmer does not react adversely. Max glances at Farmer and then Samantha. "Tell us more," Max demands.

Hartman is apparently the expert when it comes to this incredible plot for global dominance and he presents his case. He begins by pointing out that the quest for ultimate power is not new, but has been misinterpreted throughout history. Even the leaders of ancient civilizations recognized the potential of the "God's" power.

The Nazis discovered the first evidence of Nomads presence in early civilizations through their hunt for archaeological treasures during World War II. They hoped to apply such knowledge to achieve the Reich's goal of world dominance. The details of the Nazi discoveries were found in confiscated files and through Operation

Paperclip after World War II. Immediately, U.S. analysts determined that some of the Nazi information was missing and likely taken to South America by the fleeing Nazis. It was also assumed that the Russians had obtained some of this same ET information from liberated files and captured Nazi scientists.

In the West, much of the information regarding intelligent ET life was initially dismissed as Nazi misinterpretations of the archaeological record and artifacts; however, it was taken more seriously after Roswell. According to Hartman, it was surmised that during the 19th and early 20th centuries, archaeologists were incorrectly attributing mythical and religious interpretations to ancient events that are now acknowledged to be flying craft, Nomads and BEEs based on current and more advanced scientific knowledge. These reassessments are classified top secret and never disclosed to the archaeological community, which explains why myth and religion endures as the popularly accepted interpretations of ancient texts, art and architecture.

Some of the information contained in the Nazi archives also raised the question of "Just how much influence have the Nomads had in the development of human kind?" Unfortunately, this is a subject that has eluded discovery and remains shrouded in mystery, Hartman concedes. "It appears someone was deliberate in omitting such information from any known records which has led to the suspicion that this is the secret safe-guarded by the Tutoribus. Nevertheless, these concerns appeared secondary to the quest for ultimate power," he adds.

Over the years few connections were made publicly between ancient history and Nomads until Eric von Däniken published *Chariots of the Gods* in 1968. Hartman explains that although publicly dismissed as wild speculation, the truth is that von Däniken was correct. In fact, von Däniken's theories were so accurate that he was secretly investigated to determine if von Däniken had access to previously undiscovered sources of information. This came at a time when reports of UFO activity had reached an all time high and there was concern within the intelligence community that the genie may have escaped the bottle. However, thanks to the ridicule of the popular media and the old philosophy, "It can't be therefore it isn't" the crisis quickly passed. Whether or not the derisive reaction from the media was staged or not was unclear to Hartman. "And if it were not for von Däniken's notoriety, the Tutoribus may have intervened to silence him," Raymend adds ominously.

"The archaeological records are one example of evidence hiding in plain sight and a perfect example of the philosophy, 'it can't be, therefore it isn't,'" Hartman points out. He is quick to concede that not all archaeological discoveries are Nomads related, nevertheless some are quite obvious. He also points out it is important to note that archaeological records and religious texts often describe Nomads in the presence of BEEs (the Greys) thus providing further evidence of the relationship between the two.

Hartman alleges that DARPA has funded a number of archaeological projects over the years in search of ET technology. This was accomplished through public proxy companies and philanthropic organizations as well as government grants from cultural and educational institutions including such prestigious groups as the Smithsonian, the National Science Foundation and the National Endowment for Humanities. The interesting part is the difference in the interpretations regarding archeological discoveries between the civilian archaeologists of record, and DARPA's archaeological teams. Conventional archaeology continues to interpret discoveries in terms of myth and religion, while the classified top-secret DARPA analyses are quite different.

Hartman explains that the objectives of the DARPA archaeologists are to find the keys to technological supremacy left by the Nomads if not actual technology. The problem has been decoding the descriptions left by early civilizations of technology beyond their comprehension. In other words, was the flaming chariot streaking across the sky in reality an aircraft or missile of some type? Are the vimanas of ancient India actually spacecraft? And, what about ancient Mayan ruler King Pakal? Does the lid of his sarcophagus actually depict the king sitting in a space capsule of some type?

The archaeological references are too numerous to ignore according to Hartman. An ancient stone figure representing the "Sky People" was found at the Mayan ruins in Tikal, Guatemala, and resembles a modern-day astronaut in a space helmet. References to the Sky People have appeared in stories throughout North and South America. The 14th century Fresco painting entitled 'The Crucifixion' depicts a man in some kind of craft looking back over his shoulder. "In hindsight, and armed with 21st century scientific knowledge, some of the metaphors are quite obvious," Hartman asserts as he pauses to clean his glasses again. Max points out, "Some people argue that is just speculation." "It's some people's job to make sure we all believe that," Hartman counters with a smirk.

There is more evidence that the Nomads shared some of their technological secrets with ancient cultures. "Some of the engineering and construction techniques used by early civilizations to erect megalithic structures have intelligence analysts quite puzzled and lead to the conclusion they must have had some assistance,"

Hartman remarks as he continues his briefing. He points out that the construction of some ancient megaliths would be difficult to replicate using current technology; that same construction would require some of the most sophisticated and powerful construction equipment currently available.

Hartman is referring to the ancient cities of Tiwanaku and Pumapunku, Bolivia where stone blocks of enormous size were cut and moved as far as 50 miles in the period 500-600 A.D. Some stone blocks at Tiwanaku weigh over 400 tons and had to be carried, pushed or dragged from a quarry some 6 miles away. Then there is the fact that no mortar was used to join the blocks in these megaliths. Even more incredible, we are asked to believe the people of Tiwanaku apparently did all this without a written language, metal tools and without the wheel, which didn't exist until Europeans arrived in the early 1500s. Hartman submits, "This is one example where the DARPA archaeologists are convinced the facts are inconsistent with the more clichéd explanation of mainstream archaeology,"

Then, as Hartman point out, that our own space exploration relies on an ability to employ the natural resources found on alien worlds to construct bases, raises the viable possibility that Nomads used a similar approach on earth thousands of years ago with the aid of their advanced science. Hartman notes that many people are familiar with the Search for Extraterrestrial Intelligence (SETI), but not so with the Search for Extraterrestrial Artifacts (SETA) and the Search for Extraterrestrial Technology (SETT) which are both variations of the SETI theme and quite active. "So, why do they let projects like SETI go on if SETI is searching for the wrong signals?" is Max's challenge. "The cost of the SETI program is deemed less significant than revealing the existence of ETs at this time," is Raymend's explanation. "Who knows? They may tap into another race," Farmer adds.

Hartman maintains that the initiatives to develop defensive technology against a possible Nomads threat held a dual purpose; they also yielded offensive weapons to achieve world "security." "Some would argue that global dominance was always the real agenda given the overwhelming superiority of ET technology. In other words, the proponents of world security supported the efforts to develop defensive weapons knowing it may be ineffective against the Nomads, but instrumental to their goals," Farmer interjects. Hartman continues by reasserting that global dominance is dependent upon control of space and the Nomads possess the tools to easily achieve that goal. This race for control of space began in the late 1950's and continues to this day despite any international treaties. As far back as the late 1960's and 1970's, efforts were underway to develop technology for global dominance using EXTECH. Raymend explains that EXTECH or EXTECH Notes is Top Secret intelligence information regarding extraterrestrial technology. The main players were initially the United States and Soviet Union aided by the knowledge of former Nazi scientists.

"Despite all the publicity in the late 1950s and early 1960s about the Soviet space program, there were many ominous secrets hidden from the public," Hartman asserts. "Activities that were not as benign as Sputnik," he adds. He recalls that in the 1960s the Soviet Union deployed a nuclear space weapon called the fractional orbital bombardment system. It employed a satellite orbiting in a low earth orbit, between 400 and 1,000 miles, equipped with ballistic missile designed to re-enter Earth's atmosphere and attack the United States by traveling southward from the Poles to avoid radar detection. "That movie, *Space Cowboys*, was not so far-fetched," Farmer interjects.

Farmer admits that the idea of an orbiting missile-based weapons platform was not a surprise; however, U.S. analysts quickly determined that this system would provide Moscow with a space-based, first strike weapon that could also be used in a devastating electro-magnetic pulse attack over U.S. territory. Hartman points out that, "Aside from the implementation of this weapon, another concern at the time was where had the Soviet's gotten the inspiration for the EM technology? Had they discovered the Holy Grail of technological knowledge, or perhaps worse, did they get direct assistance from the Nomads?" Hartman alleges that this led to a panicked Exchange with the Nomads accusing them with interfering in world affairs. Marvin was indifferent regarding the accusations, but agreed to impart the principles of EMFs and its relation to electro-magnetic radiation. The race for EM-based weapons had begun and the Nomads had the answers.

As Hartman tells it, during the 1960s the first step for the U.S. was to reexamine the Roswell material to determine what could be applied to the space program and what could be applied to weapons and defense research. He claims the real space program was a race for strategic control of space as well as tracking down Nomads on the moon. It was already known that the Nomads had a presence on the moon; however, the extent of that presence was unclear. As a result, some of the mission data and technical innovations resulting from the U.S. space program are still classified top-secret. "It was more than just Velcro," Farmer quips.

"So President Kennedy lied about the reasons for the race to the moon?" Max infers. "No, he told the truth; half of it. That's the way it is," Tucker responds. "Nomads were on the moon and we believed that the first people to the moon could establish an alliance with the Nomads, and perhaps, gain access to their technology. This was the real competition between the U.S. and Soviets," is Raymend's contention. He adds that success was considered so vital that any and all means were authorized to gain an advantage. In fact, documents still classified as top secret suggest that Apollo 13 was not an accident, but rather an act of sabotage. Even the astronauts are unaware of these reports which indicated that maintenance errors and equipment flaws were deliberately excluded from pre-flight inspection reports. The result was that repairs that could have prevented the near fatal explosions aboard Apollo 13 were not completed. Raymend comments this may have been an act of sabotage by "convenience" in that it was not planned, but when the opportunity arose, advantage was taken by foreign agents working the project whose original mission was simply espionage.

Farmer explains that the Apollo 13 Moon Mission was to land in the Fra Mauro area of the moon in April of 1970. However, an explosion on board forced Apollo 13 to circle the moon without landing. The mission was aborted after the rupture of a service module oxygen tank. More specifically, Apollo 13's Number Two oxygen tank blew up, causing the Number One tank to also fail. The command module's supply of electricity, light and water was lost while Apollo 13 was about 200,000 miles from Earth. Still, the mission was considered a "successful failure" because of the safe return of the crew and the engineering experience gained through the innovative effort. A subsequent investigation publicly announced the explosion was caused by a series of maintenance procedures that compromised an oxygen tank already afflicted by a manufacturing flaw. But now, Raymend is reporting that it was no accident.

There is a pause in the discussion when Max signals a time out. He thinks for a moment, organizing his thoughts. "You're telling us, we went to the moon in hopes of hooking up with some alien race so we could scam their technology?" Max infers seeking some type of confirmation. Hartman only stares impassively at Max in silent affirmation of what he considers an obvious conclusion. "We got there and the Soviet's didn't. So, what happened?" Samantha asks. "When we got there, the Nomads were gone. We found traces of their presence, but no Nomads. As you know we tried a number of times, but no luck and the program was canceled," is Hartman's answer. "Their dronecraft observed some of our landings so we know they were aware of our activities," Raymend adds. "Apparently, we were on our own and somehow, the Soviets had a head start," Hartman remarks. Concerns were raised that EXTECH formed the basis for some of the Soviet early weapons development. "Project Moondust and Operation Blue Fly had two objectives beyond retrieving secret U.S. space technology; determine how far the Soviets had progressed by retrieving any downed technology, and recover downed ET technology," Hartman adds.

Farmer gets up to stretch his legs. He stares out the window as he explains that by the late 1960s research on the Roswell material was beginning to pay dividends, but most of the technology was still beyond our science. He concedes that what we learned was more about concepts than applied engineering and apparently the Soviets had access to some of the same information. "It was decided we had to be more aggressive in reverse engineering the Roswell material and that's where Corso's work became beneficial," Farmer informs them as he sits down on a hay bale. Max challenges farmer, "Wait, I though you said we've had contact with these Nomads." "Contact was sketchy during the 1950s and 1960s. It became more consistent in the 1970s," is Walker's answer. "After the moon missions were canceled," Samantha muses suggesting some type of ET extortion aimed at forcing an end to the U.S moon missions. Walker affirms her observation with a nod; his face animated with a thin contrite smile and raised brows. "Now after almost 70 years we have finally made some significant progress," Famer boasts proudly. "Toward global dominance," Samantha admonishes him. Farmer nods sheepishly.

Raymend admits that the USAF Space Command doesn't hide the fact that it wants to establish U.S. supremacy in space. "If we don't do it someone else will," he argues. He refers to a report called "Vision for 2020", in which the Space Command suggests openly that space weapons must be developed to protect U.S. satellites, *and other space vehicles*, as foreign governments expand their space programs. However, Raymend alleges classified documents indicate a more wide-ranging objective specifically to develop and deploy space weapons to achieve *space superiority* as well as provide defense against potential "*non-terrestrial*" threats. To that end, there are a number of space weapons currently under development including Chemical Lasers, Particle Beams, and the military space planes. And, there are a number of programs so deeply cloaked in the shadows that even their project names are classified top-secret.

Farmer can see the confusion on Max and Samantha's faces. So, he takes a moment to explain some of the science behind the technology. He starts by explaining that chemical Lasers are lasers that involve the mixing of chemicals to create a laser beam and have been developed for both space-based and ground-based weapons. These laser systems include hydrogen fluoride (HF), deuterium fluoride (DF) and chemical oxygen iodine (COIL) based technology.

Max thinks for a moment and then questions the potential application of a hydrogen fluoride laser. He reasons out loud that a hydrogen fluoride laser would be absorbed by the Earth's atmosphere and concludes it is obviously designed to be used in space-to-space combat. "Very astute, Mr. Park," Farmer compliments Max and adds that the laser has been publicly described as a ballistic missile defensive system capable of destroying orbiting satellites that could threaten the U.S.; however, the classified documents also point out its purpose is to ensure U.S. superiority in space and deter potential "*extraterrestrial*" threats. Now, the goal of space dominance has become inseparable from the mission to acquire defensive weapons against potential ET threats, assuring the proponents of world security a means to their ends.

Raymend draws a connection between the HAARP research and space-based weapons development. He explains that most land-based HAARP arrays have been abandoned and replaced by space based arrays that can focus EM energy in any direction over both hemispheres. The problem of generating sufficient power necessary for a viable weapon has been overcome and arrays can be spread out by linking satellites and the unmanned slow moving, sensor equipped "triangles" to cover vast areas. The so-called "Black Knight" satellite was a product of the HAARP project, but was damaged by a mysterious burst of EM radiation. According to Raymend, this satellite-based system was code-named ELVIS for ELectromagnetic Van allen Interphase System. There was ELVIS 1, ELVIS 2, and ELVIS 3 in the satellite test array. It is believed that Nomads have hidden orbiting surveillance and weapons platforms amongst space junk by employing advanced cloaking technology. One of these weapons may have caused ELVIS 2 (Black Knight) to malfunction. Evidence indicates that an EM energy burst likely destroyed ELVIS 2 and neither Russia nor China was believed to have a workable device at the time.

Raymend can see that Max and Samantha are struggling to rationalize the unbelievable story being presented to them and pauses. It would be so much easier to dismiss all this if these men weren't so credible thinks Max. "Stop us when you've heard enough," Raymend says giving Max a chance to flinch, but Max does not. Raymend continues by reminding them it been determined that the Nomads can use EMFs and gravitational waves to create effects that mimic solar storms, change the trajectory of asteroids, modify the weather and cause geophysical effects such as earthquakes. "Quite useful for anyone hoping to establish a single authority on Earth," Raymend suggests slyly.

Farmer acknowledges Raymend by stating that those concepts were proven by our own EMF research during the HAARP project, but at the time we were unable to generate enough consistent power to sustain the bursts long enough to be effective. In fact, the original patent for HAARP describes its potential for weather modification. Conversely, gravitational waves are too subtle to control with current technology, but the Nomads have mastered such power. "Consider how that power could be used to create a new world order," Tucker postulates. He refers to the RAND Corporation who has stated it is a fact that an orbiting asteroid could be manipulated to impact an enemy target on Earth. But with our current scientific knowledge, the RAND Corporation also determined more effort would be required to achieve such a result than was employed to develop the first A-bomb.

Walker reveals that EM weapons have an even darker side that is arguably useful only against a human population. EMFs can also serve as a biotech, or psychotronic, weapon that can be used for mind control. In the late 1970s, the Air Force's Foreign Technology Division awarded a contract to an SRI research team to replicate Soviet psi experiments, as well as test the Soviet hypothesis that psi was transmitted via ELF (Extremely Low Frequency) electromagnetic waves. "It was subsequently discovered that these waves can also be transmitted via cell phone technology and have been employed by super secret intelligence agencies for many years," Walker remarks. But, the ultimate objective is still to learn how Nomads can tap into human consciousness, which is more physiological than mechanical. "Somehow their brains can intercept and process human thought just as though it were transmitted via radio or Wi-Fi," Walker reveals with a hint of envy.

As formidable as our new weapons might be, Farmer concedes that they would be ineffective against the Nomads based on what we know. His point being that the obvious conclusion must be that these weapons only viable purpose is to provide military superiority to achieve global dominance. A secondary motive is that some believe a single authority on Earth could lead to better relationship with the Nomads, thus encouraging them to share their secrets. The knowledge of such secrets could lead to technological advancements that would solve the world's energy problems and provide significant advances in medical science virtually eliminating disease and extending the human life span, for example. "The mission continues to be to ruthlessly acquire any information regarding Nomads technology that can be used to achieve this world 'security,' but the question remains does the ends justify the means?" Raymend muses out loud. The Nomads have shown no apparent interest in our "intra-species" power struggles other than to reclaim their technology to prevent its misuse. "They don't seem to care if we destroy ourselves through internal conflicts," is Raymend's observation.

Apparently no one, or no group, is immune from this crusade for power. "One of the most focused and darkest espionage program is aimed at obtaining ET-related information hidden in Vatican archives. The church is not without involvement in this drama," Tucker asserts. "Orbis unum," Max interjects. "Very good, Mr. Park. One World, a concept held by the church for thousands of years," Tucker compliments Max. "Some would argue it was the real objective of the Crusades," he adds. According to Tucker, the Black budget pays for this espionage program which has seen little success because the Vatican has authorized any means necessary to keep its secrets secure. "You're referring to Corvus and the Tutoribus," infers Samantha. Tucker nods affirmatively and continues.

The primary objective of the espionage program is to locate any information regarding Nomads and their technology that the church possesses, and any role the church has played in the relationship between mankind and our ET visitors over the years. While the archives may hold the secrets to the ET technology, the church doesn't possess the resources to apply it. "Thus far the church has not taken sides in the struggle for global dominance," Tucker points out. "But that could change given recent developments in the Middle East," he suggests. "But there is something else," Walker states ponderously. "We don't know what it is, but it must be incredibly significant," he speculates.

Hartman stands again and announces that "Today, just about every government is studying EMFs and EM energy and its capability." He maintains that research has proven EMFs and EM radiation can be used for propulsion, offensive and defensive weapons, geophysical modification, mind control as well as surveillance and communications, and that the Nomads hold the secrets to EMF technology. Raymend reports that as early as 1987, a Cold War Pentagon publication called "Soviet Military Power" warned that the Soviets might be close to "a prototype short-range tactical RF (radio frequency) weapon". The Washington Post also reported the same year that Soviets had used an electromagnetic weapon to kill goats at a range of about half a mile. Those projects slowed somewhat with the fall of the Iron Curtin and the economic crisis in Russia. But, in March 2012 the Russian defense minister Anatoli Serdjukov stated: "The development of weaponry based on new physics principles; direct-energy weapons, geophysical weapons, wave-energy weapons, genetic weapons, psychotronic weapons, etc., is part of the state arms procurement program for 2011-2020." And, this time the focus includes programs aimed at acquiring ET technology, from the same ETs that the world powers assure the public do not exist. It now appears that the Cold War has officially been revived with China as a new player.

Raymend points out that the Pentagon's 2015 annual report to Congress regarding Chinese military and security developments raises particular concern about China's use of directed-energy weapons, satellite jammers and other technology that can be used to take out the communications grid and weaken U.S. military positions. Raymend explains that this is because a significant element of modern military power depends on satellites for GPS and communications, early warning and even "targeting" systems. Thus it is evident these are not just defensive initiatives on the part of the Chinese. Raymend asserts these new technologies being developed by the Russians and Chinese are designed to provide first-strike capability and ensure ongoing worldwide superiority, or, global dominance!

Raymend informs them, "The military is taking this quite seriously. The Navy is retraining sailors to navigate using the old celestial techniques just in case the GPS system is compromised."

"And, if all else fails there is Archangel," Hartman boasts. It was apparent that Hartman wanted to take back the comment almost as soon as he said it. Raymend shoots Hartman an icy stare. The others react in shock at Hartman's misstep and the conversation abruptly halts. There is only silence. Apparently, this is a line they do not want to cross. "What is Archangel?" Max inquires curiously. "Archangel is just a myth, Mr. Park. It doesn't exist," Raymend shoots back sternly with an intimidating stare. Shepherd jumps in, "I think you two have a lot to consider," he says to Max and Samantha. The look in Raymend's eyes tells Max it's best to back off and Max lets it drop.

Max shakes his head in disbelief, or is it confusion, as he stands and paces. "So, let me get this straight," he begins. "You want me to believe that first; aliens exist and have come to our planet, our government knows about them, and have even recovered some of their technology. Then, we have one group of people who are trying to build weapons so we can defend ourselves against these aliens, and another group of people trying to steal alien technology to take over the world. After all that, apparently the world's religions have a secret they are willing to kill to protect," Max summarizes. There is a moment of silence. "We don't care what you believe. You came to us seeking answers. We gave you those answers. You can choose what you want to believe," Raymend replies impassively. "It can't be, therefore it isn't. Isn't that correct, Mr. Park?" Tucker quips. Max has no reply. He sits down next to Samantha on a bale of hay with his head down. He brushes back his hair and holds his head in his hands, bewildered and overwhelmed.

"So, what will you do with this knowledge? Reveal it to the world; take the responsibility for its impact while risking the ridicule for such an impossible scenario?" Shepherd asks as he opens a thermos of hot chocolate. He pours three cups of hot chocolate and hands one to Max and another to Samantha. Max and Samantha consider Shepherd's question as they sip their hot chocolate in silence, still overwhelmed by what they have learned. A few hours ago Max was blissfully ignorant to the reality of existence here on Earth. Now his life has become complicated as he and Samantha share the burden of knowing what others do not know and would probably be better off not knowing. Max and Samantha are unaware that the hot chocolate is beginning to make them sleepy. "We ask that you treat this information with the utmost discretion as you consider your answer Mr. Park and Ms. Greene," is Raymend's request. Samantha's head snaps around to catch Raymend's gaze, surprised that he knows her real name. Max is already half asleep and misses the reference. Whatever is in the hot chocolate does its job. Max nods off and Samantha follows shortly.

Shepherd gets up and shakes hands with the men. They leave knowing that if Max decides to reveal this information, the majority of people will not believe it and he will be labeled a nut. Even with Samantha's corroboration there is no evidence. But it's not likely she will reveal what she has learned. Samantha has her own secret to protect.

About an hour later Max awakens and looks around an empty stable. Samantha is asleep and leaning against him. He gently nudges her and she awakens just as Shepherd steps back into the room. "It's about time you two!" Shepherd exclaims. "What happened? Where are the others?" Max groans as he glances around the empty stable still a little disoriented from whatever was in the hot chocolate. "What others? We got stood up and you two fell asleep waiting," is Shepherd's response, but his tone sounds more instructive than responsive. "The five men that were here," Samantha challenges insolently. "The ranch hands went back to the barn," is Shepherd's answer. "Not the workers. We talked with five men about Roswell and ET," Max argues. Shepherd screws up his face and shakes his head as if he doesn't understand. "The three of us had a nice talk while we waited, but you two fell asleep," Shepherd contends. "There were five other men here," Samantha insists. "Were there? Maybe you were dreaming," Shepherd suggests sternly. "You have your recollections and that's all you'll take from here," he adds furtively.

Samantha scolds him, "Dr. Shepherd, I don't like this game you are playing." "This is no game. You have crossed into a world known only to an elite few. And, there are people who would like to see that group get smaller," Shepherd warns her. "I will do what I can for you, but silence is your best defense. Remember that when you choose to use your cell phone," he adds with the wink of an eye. Shepherd extends his arm towards the door indicating that it is time to leave. Max and Samantha exit the stable followed by Shepherd.

Max and Samantha ride in silence as Samantha drives back to Max's condo. "What do you make of all this; true, or not?" Max asks her. Samantha sighs and shakes her head in confusion. "I've seen some strange stuff, but this is over the top," she confesses. "Why would they lie?" Max counters. "That's what I can't figure out. I think Shepherd has always been straight with me, but I didn't like what he pulled," Samantha responds. She reaches into her pocket, pulls out a digital audio recorder and hands it to Max. "But it doesn't matter. Got it all on tape," she announces triumphantly. "I love you," declares

Max. Samantha is caught off-guard by his proclamation and there is an awkward moment. "Oh, well, you know. Great job!" clarifies a flustered Max. Samantha grins at him.

Max switches on the recorder. There is an audible hiss, but nothing has been recorded. "What the hell?!" Samantha exclaims in frustration. "If there was anything on here, it's been erased," Max surmises out loud. Samantha is deeply disappointed and it shows on her face. "You're still a pretty cool chick," Max says hoping to ease her disappointment. She smiles at him and squeezes his hand. "I'm going to check out Mr. Shepherd and those other guys," she promises.

Samantha stops at the curb in front of Max's condo. He can see she is still disappointed. "Hey, it's okay. We'll figure this out. Do you wanna come in?" he says trying to comfort her. "No, thanks. I have some work to do," she says and kisses him on the cheek. Max has his own concerns, but figures it's best to let Samantha go now, and work it out with her later. Besides, Max has his own research to do. Max gets out of the car and watches as Samantha waves and drives off. Max heads into the condo and closes the door. A few minutes later, a car moves into position just down the road to watch over Max and the condo.

THE SCIENCE PROJECT

Samantha returns to her office at GTC. She enters a small windowless room and closes the door. The room is sparsely furnished with a gray steel desk on which sits a single computer and a note pad. This is a secure room designed for accessing information from some of the most confidential databases in the world. The network connection is a secured VPN and all data flow is encrypted using a classified cube-matrix process. Samantha begins by performing a background check on each of the men from the stable. She cross-checks FBI files, social security, military records, and Interpol, but finds nothing. She even looks into real estate and driver's license records hoping maybe to find some aliases; still nothing. But, she never really believed the men had given their real names. The military men she can probably cross-match from their service records, but that could take some time. Then, she's not even sure if she wants to identify them, she thinks. What would she do with the information? She knows if she reports the meeting to the Colonel those men could be in serious trouble and possibly, grave danger.

Just to be sure, Samantha types the rank and service history for the man calling himself Phil Raymend into a classified, special access military data base. A list of names and photos appear. She works her way down the list and eventually finds a photo of the man she spoke with, but his name is not Raymend. But, he is for real! A quick examination of his service record confirms he was in a position that would give him access to the information just as he claimed. There is no reason to believe the others are not what they say they were. And, these men appear to know all about her; surely they must know she will be able to determine their identities. So, why aren't they concerned? Is that trust or arrogance, Samantha wonders? Nevertheless, it is apparent that these men are for real. For a moment, Samantha is pleased that she has confirmed the men's credibility, but just as quickly the gratification fades as Samantha realizes she may also have confirmed the stark reality of their story.

Samantha turns her attention to Dr. Shepherd. She checks the FBI files, but finds little information. She sees pretty much what she already knows. Shepherd is a professor of physics who graduated from MIT (Massachusetts Institute of Technology) in 1969. According to the records, he taught at Cal Tech and worked briefly at NASA JPL (Jet Propulsion Laboratory) in California before settling in Massachusetts. NASA's Jet Propulsion Laboratory (JPL) is a federally funded division of Caltech and the leading center for the robotic exploration of the solar system. Other than that, his career seems oddly unremarkable. Samantha finds no record of published papers or distinguishing research. The less information she finds about Shepherd, the more curious she becomes. It just doesn't make any sense for a man of his position.

Who is this man, Samantha wonders? She digs a little deeper. It appears that Shepherd was born in 1947 to Harriet and Edward Shepherd in Albuquerque, New Mexico, but Samantha finds no birth certificate. There is no information from 1947 to 1969 when records indicate Shepherd graduated from MIT. The MIT records appear in order, but there is something odd! Samantha checks the MIT yearbook for 1969. There is no photo of Shepherd nor is he referenced anywhere in the publication. Samantha checks previous and subsequent years; nothing. It could be an oversight she thinks, so Samantha decides to follow up on Edward and Harriet.

* * * * * * *

Max is stretched out on his sofa. This is not what he had in mind for his vacation he thinks, but then again he didn't really have any plans. He tries to close his eyes and take a nap, but can't help staring at the envelope lying on the table in front of him. He turns away from the envelope and buries his face in a pillow, but still cannot seem to nod off. He gets up, grabs his computer off the desk and settles back down on the sofa with the computer on his lap. He starts searching the Internet for any corroboration of the stories he heard from the men. To his surprise, Max finds it! It's all there! Maybe not in detail and sometimes only half the story just as Tucker said. But, the facts are out there if one takes the time to piece together the information from all the different sources. It appears that no one has tried to hide this evidence; however, despite the credibility of the sources, most is hearsay or anecdotal and there is little physical evidence or official records to support it – just as Tucker and the others asserted.

* * * * * * *

Back at GTC, Samantha is interrupted by a knock on the door. She minimizes the window on the computer screen to shield the information from prying eyes. Samantha opens the door and is greeted by the Colonel dressed in an ordinary blue business suit. "Sam, I heard you were here," the Colonel announces in an inquisitive tone. "Yes, I had a little research to do. Come in," she responds warily. The Colonel joins her and she closes the door. "Anything important?" the Colonel inquires as he noses around the desk for clues. Samantha decides she doesn't want to reveal what she has learned just yet. She has an odd sense that the Colonel knows more than he has told her and she is curious about his possible motive. Samantha decides to test him.

"Off the record, how much do we really know about Roswell?" she asks. "Not much more than is in the official reports. Most of the records disappeared," he replies somewhat evasively. "What if I told you I met a vet who says it all happened?" she counters. The Colonel's head snaps around and his demeanor turns serious. "Any evidence?" he shoots back. "No," responds Samantha weakly. The Colonel's disposition softens. "I wish I had a nickel for all the Roswell stories we hear. Did you get a name?" he asks deviously. Samantha shakes her head indicating she did not. "I didn't think it important," is her excuse. "Next time, get a name. It couldn't hurt," the Colonel advises. Samantha agrees with a nod. "How's it going with Shepherd and the other guy?" the Colonel inquires. "Slow," she responds. "Keep me advised," the Colonel orders. The Colonel's volatile reaction may be the best evidence Samantha has that the men were telling the truth. Now she wonders about the Colonel's motive. What side is he on? Or, is he just protecting some national security issue of which she is not aware? Or, even more disturbing, is it possible the Tutoribus have a hand in this.

Their discussion is interrupted by another knock at the door. Samantha glances at the Colonel and then opens the door to find Carbonetti. "I heard you two were here. Anything I should know?" he inquires suspiciously as he edges past Samantha and into the room. There is a moment of uneasy silence. "No, just socializing," is the Colonel's explanation. "I was just finishing up an expense report," Samantha adds. "Good to see you, Sam," the Colonel says and leaves without any further acknowledgement of Carbonetti. Samantha smiles coyly at Carbonetti. She knows he doesn't believe their story, but she doesn't trust him either. Carbonetti glares at her and then leaves in obvious frustration. Samantha closes the door and thinks about what has just happened. The Colonel had a definite reaction to her Roswell inquiry and his attitude towards Carbonetti was dubious at best.

Carbonetti loiters in the hallway for a moment pondering the conversation with Samantha and the Colonel. The whole situation seemed odd to him. He's sure they were hiding something. Carbonetti trusts Samantha and the Colonel less than they trust him. He strides down the hallway and into his office. Carbonetti closes the door and locks it for privacy. He pulls out his cell phone and starts to dial, but thinks better of it and lays the cell phone on his desk. His cell phone has a special scrambler so no one can determine who is speaking or what is being said, but he is concerned it may be possible to determine the location from where the call originated.

Carbonetti slips on his suit jacket, grabs his cell phone and heads out the door. Carbonetti nods to the guard in the lobby as he passes through. He leaves the building and leisurely walks to his car. He climbs into his car and drives out of the parking lot. Carbonetti drives for a mile or two and finds a convenient parking lot outside a grocery store. He parks, and after a sideways glance to be sure no one is watching, pulls out his cell phone and dials.

Across town Corvus is working in his office when his cell phone rings. He grabs it and checks the number. Recognizing the number as Carbonetti, he answers, "Yes?" He pauses to listen as Carbonetti tells his story. "Yes, that seems odd. What do you think it means?" Corvus asks. Corvus eyes narrow and his expression indicates he is not happy with the answer. He had hoped this problem would fade away in the fog of UFO conjecture like so many others. "I will look into it," Corvus responds coldly and ends the call. Corvus places his cell phone on the desk, picks up his desk phone and taps in a number. "Mr. Gideon, I need to see you," he says. Carbonetti lays his phone on the passenger seat of his car and drives out of the parking lot.

Samantha's suspicions paid off. She has been watching Carbonetti from across the lot and wonders what all this means? Why would Carbonetti leave the office just to make a phone call? When she joined the special investigations unit she never dreamed she would be working on a project like this. While never a skeptic about ETs, she was neither a true believer, but over the past year she has discovered some compelling evidence and examined top secret files that changed her perception. Samantha had heard the stories about espionage and secret societies, but had never come face to face with those realities. Now, confronted with the situation at hand, it all seems too fantastic even to her to be true; but it is. And the danger has become very real. She realizes that Max's life really is in danger! This situation has gotten too far beyond crazy and Samantha feels it's time to talk to Max.

* * * * * * * *

Max is sitting on his couch watching TV with the computer on his lap. He has decided to do a little research on Samantha. He trusts Samantha, but everything has happened so fast he realizes that he really knows little about her. His first step is to learn more about Samantha Freeman. Max is a smart guy, but unfortunately does not have the resources or the authority to access any information other than is publicly available on the Internet.

He types in "Samantha Freeman" and learns what he already knows. Samantha Freeman works for Giga Technology Consulting providing information technology consulting, and she manages a web site regarding the UFO phenomenon, and Roswell in particular. It is what Max doesn't find that raises his curiosity. With most people one would expect to find some basic background information like schools attended or maybe some birth records. So far, he sees no such information regarding Samantha. Max checks the state judicial web site to see if there are any criminal or civil cases involving Samantha. He finds nothing and considers that a good sign. Max pauses for a moment and then closes down the computer. He likes Samantha and decides to play this out, but that doesn't mean he won't be careful. From what Max has observed, Samantha is as perplexed as he. He turns his attention back to the TV and finally nods off.

Max is asleep when his cell phone rings and it startles him awake. He answers while still half-asleep. It's Samantha calling and she sounds upset. Samantha urges Max to meet her at the food court in the Burlington shopping mall. "What's wrong!" he asks with concern. "I found some more information. Please just meet me. And, bring the envelope," she pleads. Max senses the urgency in Samantha's voice. Now his concern turns to Samantha's safety. "Are you OK?" he asks with alarm. "Yes, yes, just do this for me!" she begs him. This is strange he thinks, but considering the way the day has gone, he should not be surprised. Strange as it seems, it might be the most rational thing he has heard. He agrees to meet Samantha. Max hangs up, grabs his jacket and rushes out the door with the envelope. It is getting dark as Max jumps into his car and races off. As he drives down the street, the car that has been standing watch outside his condo pulls out behind him and follows.

Samantha is sitting at a table in the center of the food court surrounded by a maze of tables and their diners. Her cell phone chirps and she answers. It is the agent in the car tailing Max. "No. He is meeting me. You're relieved," she says and hangs up. The food court is getting busy when Max arrives and he spies Samantha sitting alone at the table in the center of the dining area. He winds his way through the labyrinth of tables surrounding her. Even from a distance Max can see Samantha appears upset. This is definitely contrary to her normal calm and collected demeanor Max thinks.

Max sits down alongside Samantha with a sideways glance to see if anyone is watching them. "Are you okay?" he asks apprehensively. "No. No, this is getting out of control," she replies anxiously, her eyes wide. "I know it's pretty weird, but-" Max begins, but Samantha interrupts him. "I'm really worried about you!" she exclaims. "Hey, I can take care of myself," says Max who is still unaware of the true seriousness of his predicament. Samantha reaches out and takes Max's hands. She takes a deep breath, stares into his eyes and reveals her true identity to him. "I have to tell you something! My real name is Samantha Greene and I'm an officer in the United States Air Force. I'm a member of a top secret group assigned to investigate UFO stories," she confesses.

Max pulls his hands from Samantha's grip and stares at her with an expression that is as much confusion as disappointment. "So, this WAS all a game to you! I thought you.." he says forlornly. He is genuinely hurt and Samantha can see the anguish in his eyes. "I'm an idiot. I thought you.." he stops again, rises and abruptly walks away without giving Samantha a chance to explain. "Max, Max. Wait!" she pleads, but Max does not respond. Samantha chases after him shoving chairs aside. She grabs his arm. Max turns and they are face to face. "No! Since the first day I met you I wished I was just Samantha Freeman. I don't want anything to happen to you!" she exclaims with tears in her eyes. Max stares into her eyes. "I'm sorry," Samantha apologizes. Max wraps his arms around Samantha and kisses her.

"Okay, now that we got that straight, what's our next move?" he asks roguishly. "Let's give the documents to Shepherd and forget the whole thing. Let's go on a vacation somewhere," Samantha suggests enthusiastically. "What? You wanna turn back now?" he counters in disbelief. "Wait! You want to continue with this?" Samantha responds apprehensively. "You're crazy! We could be in real danger!" she argues. "As long as we have those documents, they can't hurt us," Max reasons out loud. Samantha pauses and takes a deep breath. It's against her better judgment, but "Maybe we should go see Dr. Shepherd," Samantha suggests with a fragile smile. Max and Samantha make for the exit. Unknown to Max and Samantha, Mr. Gideon has been watching the whole episode from a table far on the fringe of the food court. He pulls out his cell phone and makes a call.

Max drives and Samantha reveals what she found, or rather did not find out about Shepherd. Samantha directs Max as he drives for about 45 minutes to a suburban neighborhood just outside Boston. They park alongside the curb in front of a white, two-story Colonial-style house with a manicured lawn and white picket fence. It is so conventional, it is a cliché. Max and Samantha hurry up the front walk and knock on the door. Dr. Shepherd answers the door and appears a bit surprised to find them, but maintains his usual composure. "I'm sorry to bother you, but we need to see you," Samantha demands.

Shepherd hesitates for a moment and glances over his shoulder, but then invites them in with a sweep of his hand. They enter into a classic living room accented by a large, bay-style picture window that overlooks the street. The home is neat and comfortable. The inside is as cliché as the outside furnished with a traditional sofa and loveseat positioned adjacent to a fireplace, and separated by a coffee table. A fire crackles in the fireplace. Max examines some of the items on the wall. A replica of the Mayan calendar hangs on one wall flanked by doctorate degrees. A Native American Kachina doll stands on the coffee table. "Please sit," Shepherd suggests congenially, "Can I get you anything?" "No, thank you," Samantha responds for the both of them. Max notices there are two empty cups on the table, but says nothing. Outside, Mr. Gideon drives past the house and parks on the side of the road about a block away. He makes a call on his cell phone.

Max and Samantha sit side by side on the sofa and it is apparent to Shepherd that they are uneasy. "You're concerned about something," Shepherd infers. "I've been looking into your background and it raises some questions," Samantha responds inquisitively. "There is no record of either Edward or Harriett Shepherd. Or, of you between the years 1947 and 1969," she points out. Shepherd smiles slyly and thinks for a moment. He looks Samantha square in the eye. "Is that Samantha Freeman asking or Capt. Greene?" he responds provocatively. "Whichever one can get an honest answer," she counters un-intimidated by his impudence. Shepherd is reluctant to answer and glances off towards an adjacent room again as if receiving direction from an unseen party.

A figure appears from the next room. He is a tall, light-skinned man with neatly cropped blonde hair. In all respects he appears to be Norwegian, but there is something different about him. It's not physical though he is a handsome man by any standard, but Max and Samantha can actually feel his presence. And, he seems to be aware of their thoughts. It is difficult to describe, but some kind of kinesthetic communication. Not only can they see and hear images and speech in their mind, but also feel it. And, it is not so much as seeing and hearing, but a sensation.

Max and Samantha are spellbound. The man doesn't introduce himself, but somehow they already know what he is. "Does my presence surprise you? You are not alone in this Universe," the Man declares coyly, speaking in flawless English. Max is awestruck and a bit unsettled by the being standing before him. Shepherd introduces the man as Mr. O'Ryan. "Mr. O'Ryan is from very far away. He is the proof that you seek," Shepherd announces wryly. "Is this a gag? Who are you?" Max snaps. O'Ryan does not respond. Max and Samantha sit in stunned silence, momentarily too mesmerized to move. Samantha gathers herself and asks O'Ryan, "Why are you here?" Shepherd interjects, "They have been here for generations." "That doesn't answer the question, 'Why?'" Max counters.

O'Ryan provides an answer. He explains that like earth, their civilization grew faster and larger than their world could accommodate comfortably. They needed to learn how to adapt their species and resources or risk extinction. Earth was a primitive world with primitive life forms and provided a suitable ecosystem for their research. "So you decided to study us!?" Samantha infers. "No. We, created you; to test our theories on the adaptability of species and ecosystems. The similarities between us are not by accident," O'Ryan reveals. Max and Samantha are dumfounded. This is impossible Max thinks.

According to O'Ryan, some of Earth's creatures were transplanted from other worlds. Some were genetically mutated from earth's primitive inhabitants. And, some, like humans, were complete genetic redesigns. "To be precise, what you refer to as genetics and DNA we call an organic matrix which allows us to duplicate life functions and fabricate cognitive processes. Similar to the way in which you program a computer," O'Ryan proclaims quite matter-of-factly. "We recognized that in order to simulate a suitable ecosystem for our research we would need to introduce living entities similar to ourselves," he adds. Max stares at O'Ryan for a moment and then shakes his head in disbelief. O'Ryan continues, "Hominids offered the best platform, but early hominids were physiologically and intellectually inferior. We had to accelerate the evolutionary process to achieve a suitable proxy for our studies."

There is more. O'Ryan reveals that human development began with alien hybrids, non-human inter-breeding experiments which were abandoned in favor of the genetically operated design. According to O'Ryan, genetic engineering allows for quick and easy reprogramming and yields a self-actualizing entity that grows and develops with little intervention. The human thought process was designed to allow the Nomads easy access for monitoring human development and activity. "However, for some reason, human cognition has not yet developed sufficiently to synchronize with the universal consciousness," states a puzzled O'Ryan.

"They call it the 'Sun' project. Over time 'adjustments' were made by providing 'developmental' guidance to selected cultures or by 're-engineering' our DNA and the Earth's ecosystem," Shepherd adds. Samantha ponders his statement for a moment. "Sun, Latin for phoenix or rebirth. Sun Gods! Those theories about alien involvement in earth's history are true!" Samantha reasons out loud. Shepherd nods implicitly. He hands Samantha some photos he retrieves from a drawer in the coffee table. Samantha examines the 5x7 black and white images of the megaliths at Tiwanaku and Pumapunku and Major Jesse Marcel. Shepherd picks up the Kachina doll and hands it to Max. "'They' are the reality to our legends and myths," Shepherd attests referring to O'Ryan and his Race. "Our influence is quite obvious back to the most ancient of your civilizations," is O'Ryan's contention and adds, "But mankind chooses not to accept that. 'It can't be' is the conventional wisdom." "Some of our greatest spiritual leaders, statesmen, explorers, as well as inventors and even scientists like Da Vinci and Einstein were 'influenced' by them," Shepherd asserts. "Da Vinci's missing time was not wasted," O'Ryan intimates.

Max examines the Kachina doll. A Kachina doll is a representation of a spirit being in certain Native American religions. This includes the Native American cultures located in the southwestern United States, such as the Hopi, Zuni, Acoma Pueblo, and Laguna Pueblo. Kachina dolls are small dolls carved in the likeness of kachinas and given to children as gifts. Shepherd explains that Kachinas are spirits or personifications of things in the real world. A kachina can represent anything in the natural world or metaphysical state, and some display a striking resemblance to beings wearing a space helmet, like the one Max is holding. Kachinas can vary by community. There are kachinas for the sun, stars, thunderstorms, wind, corn, insects, and many other entities including the Sky People. Kachinas are not worshipped, but each is viewed as a powerful being that, if given veneration and respect, can use his particular power for human good, bringing rainfall, healing, fertility, or protection, for example. Some have described the central theme of the kachina is the presence of life in all objects that fill the Universe. "Everything has an essence or a life force, and humans must interact with this essence or fail to survive. What you hold in your hand is a likeness of my ancestors created by your ancestors," O'Ryan explains.

Max challenges Shepherd, "How do you know all this is true?" Shepherd hesitates. He has a secret that he is reluctant to share, but a nod from O'Ryan encourages him to reveal his past. "I was offered the opportunity to participate in their studies after Roswell. My real name is Dr. Edmund Kiss," Shepherd confesses. "You were a member of the Waffen S.S. during World War II!" Samantha exclaims. Shepherd is agitated by the remark. "I wore the uniform for the sake of my work! The tribunal found me innocent," Shepherd counters aggressively. "Academia scoffed at your theories on Tiwanaku and Pumapunku," a bemused Samantha remarks. "As you can see, my theories were correct and I had the proof. But after the war, I was 'persuaded' to hand over my research to your government during Operation Paperclip. Most of it was destroyed," Shepherd complains. Max interrupts, "How is this possible? You should be like a hundred years old."

Shepherd rises and leaves the room. Max and Samantha are unsure what is happening and sit quietly, their eyes darting from O'Ryan to the hallway where Shepherd disappeared. Shepherd returns shortly, fumbling with a movie projector, a screen and a 16mm reel of film. "Let me show you this film," he says. "Who else knows about this?" Max inquires as Shepherd sets up the projector and screen. "There have been others over the ages, but you are the first of your time," O'Ryan reveals as Shepherd loads the 16mm reel on the projector. "Do the men we spoke with know about Mr. O'Ryan," Samantha asks trying to clarify O'Ryan's response. "No. But Mr. Raymend has his suspicions and may have shared them with the others," is Shepherd's answer.

Shepherd starts the projector. It whines and ticks as the brittle old film winds through the sprockets. Max is still spellbound by O'Ryan. "Please focus your attention on the screen," Shepherd instructs them. Moments pass before Max can wrestle his eyes away from O'Ryan. The film is vintage black and white, and a bit grainy. It shows a man in a lab coat and a CIC agent in a baggy business suit, circa 1947, standing over a desk with bits of broken sticks and wires, and some papers. Shepherd explains the man in the suit is an agent of the CIC (Counter Intelligence Corps) and the film was made as a record of their activity.

"All this material and the other debris as well as copies of these reports must be sent to Wright," the CIC Man in the suit orders. "And Washington?" the man in lab coat asks. The CIC man picks up one report in particular. "Not yet. The fewer copies the better. And we'll need to purge any log entries and activity reports. This will cause a worldwide crisis if not handled properly. Ramey will address the public announcement," the CIC Man asserts. The other man nods and responds, "I'll take care of it". The grainy picture clears a bit and the likeness between Shepherd and the man in the film is undeniable. Samantha and Max stare at Shepherd in disbelief. "Dr. Shepherd?" Samantha gasps. "OK. This has to be some kind of hoax. It's impossible!" Max exclaims. He glances at Samantha, but her expression remains serious. Max stares down Shepherd, "How? That film must be a fake," Max protests.

"I am a product of their re-engineering. Our friends made the necessary adjustments to my physiology to extend my life," Shepherd reveals referring to O'Ryan. Samantha hands the photos to Max and he studies them. "To use terms that you can understand, we have mastered a kind of 'nano' technology at the DNA level that allows us to reprogram your physiology," explains O'Ryan. Max gets up and paces. He spent eight years in a Catholic school and this contradicts everything he has been taught. Are these people the "Gods" to which the Bible and other sacred texts refer? Is this the missing link in Darwinism, Max wonders? He is momentarily stunned as he searches for a sense of identity.

"We met some men. They say our government communicates with your people. Is that true?" Samantha asks O'Ryan. "It is true," is his answer. "Then why won't you share more of your knowledge. It could be of great benefit," Samantha pleads. "Those men also explained there are people who would use such knowledge to change the world and it would interfere with our objectives. But, it is all irrelevant. You do not possess the capacity to understand," O'Ryan argues. "Try me," Max boldly challenges O'Ryan. O'Ryan nods in acceptance of the challenge and asks, "What are your questions?"

"Where are you from?" is Max's first question. "We share the galaxy," O'Ryan answers evasively. "Not much of an answer," Max admonishes O'Ryan. Max tries again. "How did you get here? How is it possible to travel great distances through space?" "The men you spoke with are basically correct. Travel is dimensional and the secret is mastering what you refer to as electromagnetic forces and manipulating gravitational waves," is O'Ryan's answer.

As O'Ryan explains it, Farmer was basically correct in his account. All matter, organic and inorganic, has an electromagnetic signature that is similar to DNA. O'Ryan contends that altering that signature allows for the manipulation of gravitational fields and many forms of electromagnetic energy. EMFs can also be used as containers or vessels to hold all forms of energy, can bend light and space, and provide barriers, or force fields. "Gravitational waves can also produce energy bursts as they accumulate, what we call cycles," O'Ryan reveals. These cycles can be used to propel spacecraft. "Think of waves on the ocean. Like the ocean's waves, gravitational waves can be used to push and pull a vessel," O'Ryan offers as an example. Likewise, he adds that Rogue or larger gravitational waves occur when smaller waves accumulate, and, gravitational waves can conflict with other waves and objects in space resulting in gravitational gyres and eddies just like in an ocean. This swirling energy can entice the rotation of all matter, even celestial bodies and black holes.

The lesson continues. O'Ryan points out that earth science assumes space travel requires great speed, but that is incorrect. Actually, it is just the opposite. A state of near absolute zero is required. If one could remain in one place one would see the movement of the Universe. But one cannot remain motionless because we are all part of a physical system pushed and pulled by gravitational forces. The Universe is constantly expanding and dimensional space is always moving and twisting just as Einstein predicted. And, all matter moves within a universal range of kinetic motion relative to the speed of light; think of it as a cosmic standard velocity (CSV), suggests O'Ryan.

"For example," O'Ryan continues, "Consider driving a car at high speed along a fence that separates two fields. There are gaps in the fence at regular intervals. At high speed the fence appears to be a solid barrier. Slow down and the gaps become visible. Go slow enough and it will be possible to pass through a gap and into the other field. In terms of the Universe, the fence is a dimensional barrier and the fields are dimensions or planes within a dimension. Gravitational ripples can be like the breaks in the fence. You must begin thinking multi-dimensionally O'Ryan lectures. Electromagnetic forces can be used as a damper against gravity as well as for propulsion in dimensional space by manipulating the push and pull of gravitational fields. However, it requires a precise procedure to get near enough to absolute zero, where the charged particles of an electromagnetic field behave differently, minimum CSV, to slow all motion without achieving absolute zero," O'Ryan concedes.

This actually makes some sense to Max. He reasons out loud that atoms are always in motion because if they became stationary, they couldn't function and pretty much wouldn't exist. This is why absolute zero can never be obtained. "To stop all motion is to stop all time, which is impossible and would be equivalent to the destruction of the Universe," Max concludes. "That is basically correct, Mr. Park," O'Ryan agrees with a hint of admiration.

Max becomes agitated. "So, we're just lab rats. Is that the explanation behind all this abduction stuff," Max scolds O'Ryan. "Your people believe too much of what they see in your own movies. We have no need for abductions. No need for physical contact, but the idea seems to intrigue the human psyche," is O'Ryan's response. "Apparently our design has successfully provided the capability for faith and obstinacy considering some human's unwavering belief in alien abduction stories," observes a mildly amused O'Ryan. O'Ryan clarifies by suggesting Max and Samantha consider human consciousness as just one frequency in an infinite number of frequencies in the general consciousness of the Universe. Human consciousness is very primitive and easily tapped by more sophisticated life forms. "We can simply 'tune' our minds into human consciousness as we choose to gather any information we may need," O'Ryan explains quite nonchalantly. "Einstein's unified theory was correct," Samantha proclaims. "He was one of the privileged few, like Dr. Shepherd," O'Ryan confesses.

"Is it true that what we call the 'Greys', are biological creatures that you created?" Max asks. O'Ryan says nothing, but it is apparent something is happening. It is difficult to describe. It's like a sensation and an image that appears in Max's head. As if he is involved in some type of communication. He hears no voices in his head, nor does he actually see any images, but something is definitely happening. Max glances at Samantha and the wide-eyed expression on her face indicates she senses it too.

Slowly, silently, a small figure appears from out of the next room. It seems to be walking, and at the same time, gliding across the floor. It is a Grey alien about four feet tall with a large head, slight body and large, black almond-shaped eyes! Max and Samantha are awestruck; it is one of the BEEs of whom the men spoke. Max and Samantha watch as he moves silently and stops in front of them, his black, lifeless eyes fixed on them. O'Ryan and Shepherd are amused by Max and Samantha's reaction to the otherworldly creature.

"This is a biological proxy," O'Ryan explains. "I call him Simon," Shepherd quips. "Does this sufficiently answer your question, Mr. Park?" O'Ryan asks rhetorically. "If you would like to communicate with Simon, clear your mind and focus on him. Your minds are not sophisticated enough to initiate communication, but he will tap into your consciousness and establish a link with you," O'Ryan instructs Max and Samantha. Max glances at Samantha, and then Shepherd, and hesitates. Samantha is as confused as Max and unsure what to do next; she only shrugs. O'Ryan immediately senses their reluctance. "Do not be concerned. He will not harm you," O'Ryan assures them.

Max is not sure if O'Ryan verbally spoke the words or not, but the message was received.

Max and Samantha focus their attention on Simon. They suddenly feel lightheaded. It clears quickly, but they are not the same. They feel different somehow. In the blink of an eye this creature has provided them with the knowledge regarding the nature of its existence. This is not a gradual learning experience, but a sudden awareness. Max and Samantha now share the knowledge that these creatures are not genetically operated designs as are humans. Max and Samantha's minds are awash with images, sounds and sensations. Separately they are unintelligible, but together represent unimaginable knowledge.

The Greys do not grow, but they are alive by human standards. They are organic, assembled in the same way we would assemble a robot, but using a more sophisticated process and materials. Upon completion they can be "organically programmed" for any mission. They are super-intelligent with a built-in "archive" of advanced knowledge they can draw upon to support any mission. Their minds are basically organic super-computers. That way, the Greys can be reprogrammed for just about any mission. They are electrically powered just like the human body, but do not have a specific personality nor do they have emotions. The Greys are beings of pure logic; however, they do have the capability to understand and predict human behavior and emotion. They do not die in the sense human beings die, they just cease to function. These creatures can be repaired and revived. As in the case of Roswell, the "dead" BEEs (Greys) were returned in exchange for ongoing communication with the Nomads. Simon also intimates that humans can be revived or repaired as well, but it is a more complex process. Simon is referring to restoring life from death! Max and Samantha know all this just as clearly as they know the alphabet.

Samantha stands, reaches out and gently touches Simon's head. He does not react and there is no sense of emotion, fear or otherwise, from him. He is cool to the touch. His "skin" has a smooth, very fine, grainy feeling. He stares at her with those black eyes. She senses that Simon is trying to interpret the purpose of her touch. Just as quickly she senses that Simon has attributed her actions to human curiosity, but still there is no emotion. Samantha sits back alongside Max.

Max suddenly realizes that, the "how" of Simon's creation has been omitted from all this information. The details of the science behind the miracle have not been revealed and Max suspects it is not an oversight. There must be a reason and Max turns to O'Ryan for an answer. O'Ryan senses Max's aggravation. O'Ryan wants Max and Samantha to understand his people's capabilities, but is not willing to share the secrets. Max now understands how ancient humans could have viewed these people as Gods. O'Ryan intercepts Max's thought and quickly points out that they are not Gods. "As powerful as we may seem, our capabilities are quite insignificant to those of the creator," O'Ryan concedes.

Somehow through this general consciousness Max knows that Samantha has received the same message. Max and Samantha glance at each other. In this enlightened state, Max not only sees her glance, but feels it. It is a warm and comforting sensation. He can feel her emotions towards him as well as her reactions to O'Ryan and Simon. It seems to be all one stream of consciousness, but at the same time separate emotions. This type of power is beyond comprehension they concede and realize O'Ryan has made his point. Max also realizes the real question has become, "What can't they do?"

Human existence suddenly appears inconsequential compared to this greater intelligence and Max and Samantha are filled with a sense of insignificance. O'Ryan looks at them caringly, like a father looks at a frightened child. His reaction is reassuring and comforting. No words are spoken and there are no images, just a warm and comforting sensation. "Will we ever achieve your level of existence?" Samantha asks O'Ryan. There is a definite sense of hesitation from O'Ryan, which confuses and concerns Max and Samantha. O'Ryan only gazes at them. Suddenly, Max and Samantha sense something is wrong. It is a dark sensation and the message seems scrambled. The link between O'Ryan, Simon, Max and Samantha is abruptly severed. Shepherd has sensed the same disturbance and rushes to the window. "We have company," he announces.

THE CONVERGENCE

Max joins Shepherd at the window. He watches as two black sedans park at the curb in front of Shepherd's house and two men in black suits step out of the cars. Corvus has arrived with Mr. Gideon. Corvus glances up at the house and sees Max in the window with Shepherd. Corvus' eyes meet Max's. "Who is that?" Max asks. "That is Corvus," Shepherd responds ominously. Samantha overhears and rushes to the window to get a look at Corvus. She will finally get to meet the man she has sought, she thinks.

What Samantha has learned tells her this is a dangerous man and this is not a social call. She puts her foot on a chair, slides up her pants leg and pulls out her weapon. She releases the magazine, checks it and slides it back into the handle of the pistol with a click. Max stares at Samantha with wide eyes and a furrowed brow revealing his surprise at learning she is packing. She tucks the pistol back into the holster and notices Max staring at her. "You can't be too careful," she confesses sheepishly. "Let us hope that won't be necessary," Shepherd chides her.

They move away from the window and back into the living room awaiting Corvus arrival. Max knows little of Corvus, but what he has heard makes Max believe Corvus is looking for him. Max still has a chance to take Samantha and slip out the back door. What the hell, I'm only a financial consultant. I'm no secret agent, he thinks to himself. But, if it is adventure Max is looking for, it just arrived.

And if what they have said about Corvus is true, Max knows Corvus would only hunt him down. Plus, this is Max's battle not Samantha's. Max turns to Samantha, "Why don't you slip out the back," he suggests to her. She takes his hand, stares him in the eye, and without hesitation firmly replies, "No". In the excitement, O'Ryan and Simon have slipped away leaving only Max, Samantha and Shepherd to face off with Corvus and Mr. Gideon.

Samantha has her own concerns. She is well aware of Corvus' history, but what of Shepherd? The gaps in his background leave her unsure of his agenda or where his allegiance lies, so she cannot be sure of what Shepherd will do next. A few moments pass and there is a knock at the door. It is a heavy and menacing rap. Shepherd glances at Max and Samantha, his forehead creases, silently inquiring if they are ready, and then opens the door.

Corvus stands in the doorway flanked by Mr. Gideon. Corvus is an imposing, stone-faced figure who fills the portal. He does not wait to be invited inside and brushes Shepherd aside as he enters. Mr. Gideon follows brusquely. For a moment Corvus says nothing and surveys the room and its occupants. Mr. Gideon breaks from the group and checks the other rooms for any occupants. Max, Samantha and Shepherd stand before Corvus in tense silence. Mr. Gideon returns and edges behind Max and Samantha. He shakes his head signaling to Corvus that he has found nothing and positions himself, menacingly, behind Max and Samantha. Samantha turns and glares at Mr. Gideon, then returns her attention to Corvus. Max is a bit confused as to where O'Ryan has disappeared, but that is not his immediate concern.

Corvus closes the front door and confronts the group as he paces leisurely. "Interesting, finding you all here, yet quite fortuitous.

Mr. Park, I would like a word with you," he drones ominously. "Corvus, I've been told a man was murdered and his personal property stolen," Shepherd interrupts. Corvus shows no emotion. "Regrettable, but necessary in service to the church. He was uncooperative," Corvus replies and then warns Shepherd, "You are not my concern. Do not intervene." Corvus stops and turns his attention to Max as Mr. Gideon levels a 9mm pistol on the group.

Max steps away from Shepherd and Samantha, and squares off with Corvus. "You've been using faith to blind people from the truth," Max accuses Corvus. "I see you have escaped the world of illusion," Corvus replies. "The world you seek to preserve. A state of mind to keep people from knowing the truth," Max protests. "I have chosen to protect the people from the horror that is the truth, I do not blind. I shield," Corvus counters. "Everyone deserves to know that we are not the children of God, but the creation of a higher intelligence," Max argues, and at the same time confirms the stories he has heard. "Most would rather not. The knowledge you hold must never be shared," Corvus asserts and he slips a gun out from under his jacket. "That doesn't give you the right to murder," Samantha snaps at him. "I am not interested in your opinion. Now, Mr. Park, give me the material that I seek and we will leave you in peace," Corvus demands. Max shakes his head defiantly. He knows this is the only evidence that he, or apparently anyone, has to prove this story is all true. "Then we are at an impasse," Corvus declares as he pulls back the hammer on his gun with a click. "You won't get away with this. People will be looking for us," Samantha warns Corvus. "No one knows of this little meeting and Carbonetti will deal with any questions that may arise," Corvus counters confidently.

Suddenly Max is paralyzed and it is apparent from the expressions on the others faces that they are as well. Interestingly, Max realizes that he is not physically paralyzed, but it's as if his thoughts are not his own and whomever is doing the thinking leaves Max no will to move. He senses that the others are under the same control. "What's happening here?" Corvus exclaims. Max senses confusion and anger from Corvus and Mr. Gideon as they exchange glances. Max quickly recognizes this as the work of O'Ryan.

Gradually, Max's mind is overcome by a calming sensation and Simon enters the room followed by O'Ryan. Corvus and Mr. Gideon gaze at Simon in disbelief. "You think what I want you to think and see what I want you to see," O'Ryan calmly informs them. Simon takes the weapons from Corvus and Mr. Gideon. Simon stands before Mr. Gideon staring impassively into his eyes. O'Ryan releases the group from his control. Corvus studies O'Ryan. "Who is this?" Corvus demands. "The secret you have worked so ruthlessly to protect," Shepherd responds. "That is not possible. Your presence is no longer necessary," insists Corvus, addressing O'Ryan. "I am the absolute authority on this project," O'Ryan responds tersely. "The project concluded three years ago," Corvus argues. Max and Samantha are confused by this exchange. They are aware of the Sun project, but what does Corvus mean when he says it concluded three years ago? The Mayan calendar on the wall catches Samantha's eye and she has a revelation. "December 2012 was not meant to be the end of the world, but the end of the Sun project," she reasons out loud. Shepherd confirms her observation with a nod.

Max read about the prophecy of the Maya in his research. The Mayan calendar consists of three interlacing calendars. The most commonly known Mayan calendars are the Haab, the Tzolk'in, and the Calendar Round. But the Maya also developed what they called the Long Count calendar to chronologically track long-term mythical and historical events. The calendar is cyclical. Experts estimate it dates back to at least the 5th century B.C. and is still used in some Mayan communities.

The Mayan calendar moves in cycles and the last cycle ended on December 21, 2012. Some people interpreted that date as the day the world would end, but evidently it did not happen. That interpretation was based on the fact that the Mayan Long Count astronomical calendar was used specifically to measure long periods of time, or what the Maya called the "universal cycle". The universal cycle was calculated to be 5,126 years long. The Maya believed that the Universe is destroyed and then recreated at the start of each universal cycle. According to experts on the Maya culture, this belief is what inspired the multitude of prophesies concerning the end of the world in 2012. Scenarios suggested that the end of the world would coincide with the arrival of the next solar maximum, or the interaction between Earth and the black hole at the center of the galaxy, or, Earth's collision with a planet called Nibiru.

The Solar maximum or solar max is a normal period of greatest solar activity in the 11 year solar cycle of the Sun. During solar maximum, large numbers of sunspots appear and the sun's energy output grows by about a tenth of a percent.

According to a book published by Zecharia Sitchin in 1976 called *The Twelfth Planet*, ancient Sumerian texts identify Nibiru as the home planet of mankind's creators which passes through our Solar System every 3600 years.

Another prophecy, however, suggested that the date marked the start of a period during which Earth and its inhabitants would undergo a physical or spiritual transformation, and that December 21, 2012 would mark the beginning of a new era in human civilization. It's now apparent that the Maya were aware that some kind of an event would occur, but did they know about the Sun Project? Was this new era of transformation actually predicting the return of the Nomads, Max wonders?

"We have protected the secret faithfully," Corvus asserts as justification for his actions. "I am unconcerned with your politics and superstition," O'Ryan responds audaciously. What Corvus is referring to is that the world's religious sects have known the reality of human creation for ages. It is a secret known only at the highest levels of religious hierarchy and to the Tutoribus. Nevertheless, not long ago some of the world's religious leaders conceded the probable existence of ETs. Is this intended to prepare the world for the truth to be revealed Max wonders? The more he learns, the more Max sees that all the evidence is in plain sight if one just looks carefully for the clues. Are the religious leaders ready to take the final step and reveal the Nomads greater role in human evolution?

Monsignor Corrado Balducci was the first theologian to speak openly about the possibility of extraterrestrial life. According to Max's research, Monsignor Balducci is a respected Vatican theologian who reportedly enjoys a close relationship with the Pope. It was with the permission of the Vatican that he appeared on Italian television and conceded that extraterrestrial contact is a real phenomenon and "not due to psychological impairment". Balducci asserted that not only the "general populous, but also highly credible, cultured, and educated people of high status are recognizing more and more that this [UFOs, ET] is a real phenomenon".

Balducci proclaimed that extraterrestrial people are part of God's creation, but they are not angels nor are they devils. However, they are more spiritually evolved than mankind. Balducci described "Extraterrestrials" as humanoid beings which are like humans, with both a spiritual and a material nature, and a physical body which means that to move through space they need spacecraft. However, he concedes that the extraterrestrial's relationship between mind and matter is different than that of human kind. Balducci also stated, (or is it, revealed) that the existence of other inhabited planets is highly probable.

Balducci also asserted that the gap between the angels which are purely spiritual beings, and humans, which are beings of spirit and matter, body and soul, is too large to be natural. In other words, there is an unexplained gap. "Therefore it is highly probable that in between human kind and the angels, another life form exists, namely beings which have a physical body, but one which is more perfect than humans and influences the soul less in its intelligent acts and intentions," Balducci argued. He maintained that this assumption is supported by the ancient principle defined by Lucrezio Caro as "Natura non favit saltus" (The Nature makes no jumps), a principle which is still accepted by theologians. This principle holds there can be no gaps in human evolution. Are Nomads the missing link that science has sought? Were Balducci's statements a thinly veiled admission that the church knows that we are not the children of God as O'Ryan has indicated? And if so, is this the proof that these extraterrestrials have created mankind in their image? This all tracks with what Max and Samantha have been told by the men and O'Ryan.

In the years since the first Balducci statement, H.H., the Dalai Lama (for Tibetan Buddhism), Jewish rabbis in Israel and, the Muslim authorities of Turkey have also issued affirmative statements on the existence of extraterrestrials. No matter how carefully worded, that amounts to an admission of the existence of the Nomads for the largest Christian church as well as other world religions, Max surmises.

"How did the religious leaders learn of your existence?" Max asks O'Ryan. O'Ryan explains, "Ages ago theology was the best means for educating and mentoring humans. Humankind's unconditional acceptance of the word of the 'Gods' was instrumental in achieving the necessary results." O'Ryan goes on to reveal that over time certain leaders, the "Chosen Ones" had to be informed of their (Nomads) existence to achieve the progress the Nomads sought on a global scale without involving large numbers of the "Gods". These Chosen Ones were also provided with the technology of the Gods to increase those leaders' influence among their people. "This is where our science and your religion converged," declares O'Ryan.

O'Ryan reveals much of that accumulated knowledge was stored in ancient archives and libraries which remained under the control of religious leaders and institutions. That information also included the identity of the Gods. Unfortunately, Shepherd points out, some of the knowledge was lost when great libraries were destroyed during mankind's petty squabbles, but some of it survived in ancient texts, architecture and objects as well as the Vatican archives. So, is this the information that is the target of the Vatican espionage project to which Hartman referred, Max wonders?

O'Ryan confirms that the Bible and the sacred books of the great religions are actually journals that hold the answers to the questions concerning the relationship between man and the "Gods" and the secret's of the God's technology. For example, the Popol Vuh metaphorically defines the creation of humankind. The Popol Vuh is the story of creation according to the Quiche Maya of the region known today as Guatemala. Roughly translated Popol Vuh means "The Council Book", "The Book of the People" or, literally, "The Book of the Mat." The Popol Vuh has been referred to by some scholars as "The Mayan Bible".

O'Ryan also reveals that in addition to written texts, information was encoded in inorganic material like crystal and precious gems as well as gold objects for durability. Some ancient wall carvings are actually indices to "sacred" objects that contain data. For example, a gold tablet may be encoded with the technical information needed for creating and using the weapons of the Gods. This explains the ancient civilizations fascination with gold and jewels. It wasn't for financial wealth, but the wealth of knowledge that could be found encoded within the objects, Max reasons. "This knowledge was valued as the means toward the ancient quest for global dominance," O'Ryan proclaims.

Now it is easy to understand why gold, crystal and precious gems were so highly valued by ancient leaders, thinks Max. O'Ryan reveals that only the Chosen ones, the leaders, kings, emperors, or high priests, were provided with the tools to extract the information. The tool could be a staff or a scepter. In some cases, the chosen ones were taken away to be trained, which explains some of the accounts of ancient leaders traveling to the realms of the gods.

According to O'Ryan, the knowledge pertaining to the intellectual value of the objects was lost in secrecy and the destruction of ancient civilizations over time. As a result, the "sacred" gold and jewels became, mistakenly, coveted only for their ascribed financial value. Only the church remained aware of the intellectual value, but had lost the knowledge to extract this information. "This is where religion and reality converge. The religious axioms are partly true, but the real information has been lost in translation and secrecy because the few have sought not to share their knowledge," O'Ryan states. "The use of crystalline data sources is supported by the objects found at Roswell," Shepherd adds. "The Nazi's were correct. The secret to great power lies in these artifacts," Max surmises out loud.

O'Ryan sharply contradicts Max's observation. "You still do not understand. All matter, energy and existence are connected throughout the Universe. Your quest to master what you call our "technology" is in vain," O'Ryan lectures Max. "It is not just our technology, but our very being. We possess great power over the elements of your world because we are connected to your world and our technology through the great energy of the Universe. Our technology is a living entity, like Simon," O'Ryan clarifies. His point is that even their technology is created on an organic level complete with a universal consciousness.

O'Ryan explains, "Our space craft is alive by human standards and we communicate directly with its consciousness. There is a convergence between us, our technology and the energy of the Universe." It is that synergy of the Nomads life-energy and the Universe that makes it all work. Their craft need carry no fuel. It is fueled by the energy that drives the Universe and surrounds us. Piloting their craft is a synergy of mind and body. "It's like putting on a shoe that essentially becomes part of you, but our shoe can think and communicate," is O'Ryan's example.

"You are incapable of understanding or duplicating that connection," O'Ryan continues. Einstein's theory of a unified field was essentially correct, but even he was incapable of fully comprehending the concept, states O'Ryan. The lesson continues as O'Ryan explains that all matter and energy in the Universe exists by using opposing forces that maintain balance. If the balance is changed, objects will cease to exist in a given state. The Nomads possess the ability to tap into, and manipulate those forces. The human body created by the Nomads is an example of this balance on a micro-system level. All aspects of body function must be in balance for it to operate effectively. Too little oxygen or too much oxygen and the system fails, causing death, for example. O'Ryan's point is that the human body is designed on the same concepts as the Universe!

This dissertation has quickly moved beyond Max's level of comprehension even at this basic level. It may be true, it may not, and he has no way of knowing. But then, the last few days have been beyond comprehension. This whole experience has crossed the boundaries of impossibility. Max's mind is in a swirling state of confusion. He questions his sense of reality. Is this happening or is it one of those dreams that just seem so real? O'Ryan senses Max's confusion and Max is overtaken by a sense of calm. Suddenly the answers are clear to him. He can't translate this knowledge into words, but he understands. He also understands that human comprehension is too primitive to translate this knowledge into any form of human expression. Just as quickly as it came, the knowledge fades, but the sense of calm remains. The experience reminds Max of being half-asleep and seeing the answers to questions clearly, but then waking up and being unable to recall those answers. Nevertheless, Max is left with the sense that humankind is not as much insignificant, as it is un-evolved.

"You will give Corvus the material he seeks," O'Ryan instructs Max. Max is defiant, but knows he is over matched with O'Ryan. "You can't make me do that," he protests even though he knows O'Ryan easily can if he chooses. "The information is insignificant. Give Corvus the information and he will go away. I do not wish to see you harmed," O'Ryan commands. Max pleads his case, "You could stop him." "But I choose not to," is O'Ryan's reply. Max glances at Samantha with a mix of frustration and confusion. "This is crazy! I'll get the envelope. It's in the car," Samantha exclaims in exasperation, hoping to end the stand-off and free her and Max from this madness. Samantha squeezes Max's hand reassuringly and runs out to the car under the watchful eye of Mr. Gideon.

Inside the house they wait in tense silence. Max feels betrayed by Shepherd and O'Ryan, but knows there is nothing he can do about it. He glares at Corvus, but Corvus shows no emotion as if he always knew he would get his way. Samantha returns with Mr. Gideon and hands the envelope to Corvus. "You have what you want, but I still have the knowledge. Get out!" Max barks insolently. "You have a story to tell. A story no one will believe and no proof to back it up," Corvus sneers. Corvus nods respectfully to O'Ryan and then leaves with Mr. Gideon.

Max is resentful. "Why did you have us do that? You have no right to interfere. And, how do we know he won't come looking for us when you're not around to intervene?" a petulant Max scolds O'Ryan. "Have you learned nothing? That small bit of information is inconsequential. Corvus has his prize, but it is a false victory. And do not be concerned, I will ensure neither he nor Mr. Gideon will have any recollection of you or Ms. Greene, or of this meeting," O'Ryan assures Max. Max and Samantha's only response is to just gaze at

O'Ryan, awestruck once again by his seemingly infinite power over this world and its inhabitants.

"He has murdered innocent people and must pay for his crimes," demands Samantha. "That remains your issue, Ms. Greene. I will not be involved in such petty matters," O'Ryan responds flatly. "Why do you carry a gun and why have you deceived me?" Shepherd corners Samantha. "I'm not really an IT consultant. But I guess you already knew that, Dr. Shepherd," Samantha responds contritely. Shepherd confirms her suspicions with a nod. There is a moment of silence as Samantha hesitates, but Max encourages her with a smile and a nod. "I work for a government group called Section Four. I was assigned to find the truth behind all those UFO stories. Some of the information from past events was so secret, that the very few people who knew the truth have died and no one seems to know what happened to the evidence," she confesses. "Well, at least now we know the secret," Max infers. "You know only part and Corvus knows less," O'Ryan contradicts Max. "The conclusion to this experiment was never pre-determined. But now it appears inevitable," he adds.

THE FINAL REVELATION

"If you choose, I will share with you the destiny of humankind. You will be the first to know of your fate," O'Ryan offers, but cautions them, "This is not a gift, but a burden. You will never view a sunset in the same way!" "Really? How much stranger can this get?" Max responds sarcastically. O'Ryan doesn't share Max's sense of humor and scowls at him. Max can sense this is something very serious to O'Ryan. There is, for the first time, a strong sense of emotion from him. "I apologize," Max responds contritely. O'Ryan accepts the apology with a nod. "I do not wish to see you disappear into the shadows of time as did the civilizations before you," O'Ryan announces. Max and Samantha exchange a glance. What the hell does that mean, they wonder? O'Ryan offers them a seat with a sweep of his hand. Max and Samantha sit, side by side. This doesn't sound good.

O'Ryan explains that he is currently the lead scientist on the Sun project and one of the few ETs authorized to visit earth without specific permission. He confirms that the Sun project was scheduled to end in December 2012 as the Mayan calendar suggested; however, "It was not the end, but a time of assessment to determine our success or failure, and to decide the destiny of our creation," O'Ryan reveals.

"What!? This just gets even more unbelievable," exclaims an overwhelmed Max, who then asks O'Ryan, "So, are there more like you, watching us?" O'Ryan nods. It is true, but O'Ryan clarifies by explaining that Earth is protected by a single race that makes the decisions regarding the planet; however, other alien races of various forms have been given permission to interact and share their knowledge with humans over time. "Is that the reason ancient civilizations have so many different descriptions of the Gods?" Samantha asks. Again, O'Ryan nods in confirmation. He also admits that there have been unauthorized incursions by malicious alien races and such incidents received an immediate and severe response from his people. O'Ryan continues by explaining that he is also responsible for Nomad observers residing around the world. Others may come and go as needed. The observers are supported by the BEEs who provide technical assistance and transportation. "And, what your people have so insensitively referred to as MUTTS, are long-term research residents," O'Ryan adds. "The Nomads don't just come and go like tourists. It is a state-sponsored operation, not unlike our space program," Shepherd remarks. "We all live and work amongst humankind without detection or discord," O'Ryan remarks. Max and Samantha exchange a bewildered glance.

"So, what did you mean by our 'destiny'?" Max asks. O'Ryan hesitates and thinks for a moment before he responds. "The decision has yet to be made, but the answer can be found in your past. There have been many civilizations before you. Just now are you starting to discover some of these ancient ancestors through their archeological records. Others are still hidden in time. But, all of these cultures failed to achieve the objectives we had established. Those failures required us to reassess our theories and start over again. Some of what you attribute to geophysical or even cosmological events in Earth's past was caused by our intervention," O'Ryan reveals delicately.

Max rises and looks out the window. He sees a neighborhood lined with street lamps and homes with their lights aglow under a full moon. He becomes angry. "We're not a science project! There are billions of living, breathing creatures on this planet," Max argues. O'Ryan takes a deep breath and considers Max's words thoughtfully. "We do not wish to appear cruel, but your well-being is secondary to our objectives," he replies as tactfully as possible under the circumstances. "So it's just business! We must have some value," Max counters derisively, frustrated with O'Ryan's apparent insensitivity. "There are concerns that we have created a parasitic species. Humans have contributed nothing to this world and have only consumed its natural resources. Now we must consider the cosmic impact of our actions," O'Ryan laments. "I don't understand," Samantha responds. O'Ryan explains. "If we choose to abandon you, you may simply destroy yourselves. But, you may also become a threat to us and to others in the cosmos. You are not alone and your destiny is not exclusive to your world," he says. What O'Ryan is saying is that other civilizations in the Universe view human kind as a parasitic infestation and a solution must be determined to prevent contamination of the Universe.

Max challenges O'Ryan. "You seem to have little faith in your own creation." "Your science is immature. Some of its basic assumptions are incorrect, and you lack the capacity to comprehend your mistakes. Perhaps more importantly, humankind is paralyzed by foolish politics and ambivalent to the world around it. The species is contrary and deceitful. And, your world is dying. It is ravaged by storms and scarred by geological trauma all caused by your own hand," O'Ryan lectures Max. "So, pack up and leave. We'll deal with it," Max argues. O'Ryan chastises Max, "Only if human arrogance could be replaced by diligence. Even you, Mr. Park, lack any real motivation; financial planning is not very ambitious for a man with your education." "Aren't gods supposed to be more benevolent?"

Max counters angrily. "We are not gods. We are scientists protecting our home and families," O'Ryan responds steadfastly. O'Ryan argues they are not the only ones at fault here. He points out they designed the earth's ecosystems to be self-correcting to protect it, but humanity has disrupted the natural balance through blatant carelessness, which O'Ryan admits was unforeseen on their part. Now, the ecosystem has begun to correct the damage as it was designed to do. "The result will be cataclysmic for your kind," O'Ryan predicts.

It is a frightening revelation, but O'Ryan's words make sense. Max knows through his research that studies show the Earth's climate has changed throughout history. According to NASA, there have been seven cycles of glacial advance and retreat in the last 650,000 years with an abrupt end to the last ice age about 7,000 years ago. Perhaps not so coincidentally, this marked the beginning of the modern climate era and of human civilization. Most of these climate changes are the result of very small variations in the Earth's orbit that change the amount of solar energy the planet receives. Now Max wonders if this was natural or caused by the Nomads. "The current warming trend is of particular concern because most of it is human-induced and proceeding at an unanticipated rate," O'Ryan informs them. "Okay. I've heard the arguments about climate change. Are they correct?" Max asks O'Ryan.

"We have observed the earth as part of our study for thousands of years. The events over the last century are quite troubling," is O'Ryan's answer. "Recent changes in your climate have happened very quickly over decades, not in millions or even thousands of years as was the case in the ancient past. We did not anticipate this rate of change in our models," he confesses. O'Ryan confirms that scientists are correct about carbon dioxide and other gases being part of the problem. They restrict the transfer of infrared energy through the atmosphere and cause the Earth to warm in response. O'Ryan submits that just like the HAARP project overcharged the atmosphere with electromagnetic energy, this warming trend is overheating the atmosphere and the ecosystem is trying to counter the effects. "The system will balance itself," O'Ryan assures, and warns them, at the same time.

The signs of environmental decay are obvious according to official reports, and that appears to corroborate O'Ryan's story. NASA reports sea levels are rising according to recent studies. Sea levels have risen almost seven inches in the last century, which is nearly double that of the previous century. All major global historical temperature studies reveal that Earth has been on a warming trend since 1880. One might argue that this is a natural cycle, but most of the warming has occurred since the 1970s, with the 20 warmest years having occurred since 1981. Perhaps more significant, 10 of the warmest years have occurred during the past 12 years. Temperatures have risen even though NASA measured a decline in solar energy output throughout the first decade of the 21st century resulting in an unusually deep solar minimum in 2007-2009. A Solar minimum is the period of lowest solar activity in the 11 year solar cycle of the sun. During these periods, sunspot and solar flare activity diminishes, and often does not occur for days at a time.

Studies also reveal that it is not just ocean surface temperatures that are increasing. The oceans are absorbing so much of the increased heat, that approximately the top 2,500 feet of ocean indicate a temperature increase of about three tenths of a degree Fahrenheit since 1969. "It is true that the oceans were designed to absorb heat, but this absorption is occurring at a rate that we did not anticipate,"

O'Ryan concedes contritely. "This overheating affects the entire ecosystem. A simple example is what you call El Niño," he adds.

According to NOAA (National Oceanic and Atmospheric Administration), El Niño is characterized by unusually warm ocean temperatures in the Equatorial Pacific, as opposed to La Niña, which characterized by unusually cold ocean temperatures in the region. Fluctuations in temperature in the ocean-atmosphere in the tropical Pacific result in acute consequences which include increased rainfall across the southern United States and in Peru. This has resulted in destructive flooding and then drought, which is associated with devastating brush fires. El Niño has also been blamed for warmer than normal weather patterns across the North American continent resulting in extreme weather such as violent thunderstorms, hurricanes and tornados.

Max has seen the NASA data. NASA reports 2015's El Niño was exceptionally intense and will likely grow stronger in 2016. Based on satellite images, NASA also predicts the El Niño is shaping up to be as powerful as the one from 1997, which NASA believes may have contributed to the Great Ice Storm of 1998. It is also a fact that the number of record high temperature events in the United States has been increasing, while the number of record low temperature events has been decreasing. Max must admit one has only to watch the weather forecasts to see that. This is all getting very real he thinks.

There is more evidence. NASA has found that the acidity of ocean surface waters is increasing at a record pace. This increase is the result of humans emitting increasingly more carbon dioxide into the atmosphere and hence more being absorbed into the oceans. And, it continues to rise by about 2 billion tons per year.

The NASA reports go on to reveal evidence of the buildup of heat energy in a number of areas. The Greenland and Antarctic ice sheets have decreased in mass. Both the area and thickness of Arctic sea ice has declined rapidly over the last several decades and glaciers are retreating almost everywhere around the world including in the Alps, Himalayas, Andes, Rockies, Alaska and Africa. Satellite observations confirm that the amount of spring snow cover in the Northern Hemisphere has decreased over the past five decades and that the snow is melting earlier.

"All this has triggered the Earth's self-corrective process. The defensive system that we designed for the Earth will effect the necessary changes to return the ecosystem to its optimal range," O'Ryan warns and adds, "The weather and geophysical activity will become more volatile and extreme, and more frequent." Max has to concede there is little argument that the weather has become more unusual, but he believed it was only a natural weather cycle.

"There is another problem that we did not foresee. The earth's electromagnetic field has been damaged and may be unable to repair itself," O'Ryan announces. Now, Earth also faces destruction from cosmic killers like radiation and even meteor showers as its protective shell weakens. Any chance of survival has been reduced as a result of humankind's foolish and ignorant scientific experimentation with the earth's protective shield.

"Destruction of the electromagnetic field, pollution of the atmosphere and oceans, and unrestrained consumption of natural resources has reached a critical level. The Earth's resources are limited and its ecosystem is not indestructible. We have failed again," O'Ryan laments in an uncharacteristic moment of guilt mixed with disappointment. Max and Samantha can feel his agony, but they don't completely understand his comment. O'Ryan senses their confusion and explains, "Mars is the result of a previous experiment. The wasteland that you now explore is due in part to our arrogance," he confesses.

"For a super-race you seem to have miscalculated quite a bit when you created all this. Shouldn't you be able to fix it?" Max argues; his frustration mixed with a sense of helplessness. "It is possible, but the most effective solution requires returning this world to its original state," O'Ryan points out. "Wait, we didn't exist in the original state!" Samantha exclaims. Shepherd's eyes widen and he concurs with a nod of his head confirming Samantha's fears of the worst possible scenario. "Human's were not part of the original design. You do not belong here," O'Ryan concedes. "Is that really possible? Total destruction?" Max asks. O'Ryan pauses. "It is quite simple. In the past, we have precipitated such change by means of asteroid strikes, massive radiation, global storms and geologic events," is O'Ryan's answer.

Max is not too proud to admit that he is confused and frightened, but still he searches for an answer; something that will provide a solid reason to believe O'Ryan, or is he looking for an excuse not to believe? "Why tell US all of this if there's nothing we can do about it?" Max exclaims. "I believe you deserve to know. You also deserve to know that I accept the responsibility for this failure. I thought I had solved the problems, but the creation of life is beyond even our comprehension," O'Ryan confesses repentantly. "Do you think that confession absolves you?" Max scolds O'Ryan. O'Ryan ignores the question.

"Now, you know the whole story," is O'Ryan's response. "What will you do? Is it best to know that you are not the 'children of God?' Do 'they' want to know? Will it make a difference to know their destiny as you do?" O'Ryan challenges Max in regards to the people of the world. Max has no answers and only paces. "Our decision has yet to be made on what we will do. And when it is made, you will not know. There will be no global summit meeting," O'Ryan continues. "We do not mark time as you do. Many of your years may pass before a decision is made. But, it is possible that you have already condemned yourselves and the earth will make the decision for us," he adds ominously. "Why not explain this to the world? So we can work together to save ourselves?" Max pleads with O'Ryan. "That is not my decision to make, and even now you may not have enough time to stop the ecological correction process. Even if you were able to stop the process, it will not ensure your survival if our decision is not in your favor," O'Ryan responds almost apologetically.

"Is death the end for us?" Samantha asks almost reluctantly. She is torn between knowing and not knowing. "No, but you still can't comprehend life, so you could never comprehend death. But that also will be part of our decision," O'Ryan answers. He tries to explain that even simple life is a complex balance of energy and matter and as life becomes more sophisticated, the balance changes. The need for the matter decreases and what remains is pure energy. But not all life makes the transition to the state of pure energy. Some human life will end with the decay of the matter, or physical body. Its energy, or life force, will not be strong enough to make the transition from the corporeal dimensional state of matter to an incorporeal existence of pure energy. In that state, human consciousness continues on a separate plane from the physical dimension. It is true that in some situations the physical dimension and the incorporeal plane may intersect allowing interaction with the consciousness of those passed. It is also true the human mind is designed with the capacity for this communication but few are cognitive of the ability. "We are displeased some use this capacity for financial gain," sneers O'Ryan in an indictment of those who profess to be "psychic" mediums and a further affirmation of the dubious nature of humankind.

In human form, matter and energy, or consciousness, are inseparable, but this is not universally true. There are places within the Universe where "life" has evolved beyond that need and do not require such an amalgamation. "Even we do not possess the intelligence to create such a perfect life form. So you are the product of a simpler science," O'Ryan admits humbly. "So, what you're saying is that for some of us, death is the end, but others pass on to a new existence and you could prevent that passing," Max paraphrases. "You're insight is correct," O'Ryan responds.

Max and Samantha sit in silent contemplation. "What is your world like? Do you have a family?" Samantha asks tenderly. O'Ryan can feel her emotion and is moved by her interest in his life. Although separated by thousands of years of evolution, this human female has touched his soul. Max and Samantha can sense O'Ryan's affection for his home and his appreciation for Samantha's consideration. "My world is a lot like this one and I have a family with two children. I sacrificed my time with them to save their future. I trusted no one else. My only regret is that I may have sacrificed others, but I must not fail them," O'Ryan responds like any father would, the sense of emotion from him the strongest yet.

"Do you die," Max asks O'Ryan. "Not in the human sense and our life span is much longer, but we evolve to another state of consciousness," O'Ryan responds. It is apparent that Max and Samantha are struggling to understand, or maybe, believe all this, and O'Ryan senses it. "Do not be concerned that you do not understand. And, it may be more comforting not to believe. You cannot change what will be. Your denial is a psychological safeguard as is hope, to protect you from reality" O'Ryan explains. "Much of what you say is described in the Bible," Samantha comments. "Not just the Bible, but all religious texts. The information is of one source, but has been interpreted differently by human cultures," O'Ryan confirms.

Max and Samantha are lost in his words. "For good or bad you are a part of us. My fondest hope is that we may meet again and I will do all I can for you" O'Ryan promises and turns to leave. "Wait! Mr. O'Ryan, is there a God?" Max asks. O'Ryan pauses and with a thin smile reassures them, "There is certainly a grand architect so omnipotent that it possesses greater wisdom and power than even we can comprehend." O'Ryan and Simon disappear down the hallway.

Max still hopes that all this has been a ruse or a dream because he knows there is nothing humankind can do if not. Max has no evidence. No one would believe this story if he chose to share it and others would seek to silence him. Although Max doesn't fully comprehend O'Ryan's concept of death, he wonders if that alternative is preferable given the state of the world. O'Ryan has perhaps left Max with one piece of evidence or is it a gift? He can sense Samantha's thoughts. O'Ryan has left them with a shared consciousness.

Samantha struggles with her own issues. Her job is to report back on what she has found. But can she trust the people for whom she works? Carbonetti can't be trusted and what of the Colonel? Samantha is unsure of his true agenda. How would this information be received without any evidence? And, what if they did believe her? Would it help the people of the world, or just provide a warning to protect the elite? Then there is the question of just how deeply the Tutoribus has infiltrated the government and the military; and, what of the Nomads themselves? Samantha's best choice may be to resign her commission and remain silent. Still that could have consequences if she subsequently chose to reveal anything she had learned while on duty. Max can sense Samantha's conflict and gazes at her with a shrug and an understanding smile. He places his arm around her shoulders.

Still there is an uncomfortable feeling of loneliness. Max and Samantha alone know the biggest secret. There is no one they can turn to for comfort except each other. Max and Samantha are now the experts on the meaning of life and still they do not have any answers. They are cursed with the knowledge of knowing without the capacity to understand. What about their families? How do they share such a secret? When they look at their families and friends, what will they see? Can there be any joy in their lives now? Is life worth living if the end is pre-determined Max and Samantha wonder? And, of course there is the difference in time. What did O'Ryan mean? Was he talking days, years or millennium?

But perhaps, O'Ryan got something correct; Max and Samantha still have a flicker of hope. Hope that this all may be a dream, and hope that it could change with O'Ryan's promise of help if not. Or, just maybe, the Grand Architect of whom O'Ryan spoke will take a hand in this drama for survival of one small civilization in a magnificent creation. Max and Samantha sit in silence with Shepherd, unsure of the next step. "I think we should share this with your friends," Max suggests to Shepherd, hoping the men may offer some words of wisdom. Shepherd agrees with a nod. "I will speak with them. They will contact you if they choose."

Max shakes hands with Shepherd and Samantha hugs him. Somehow they know this is the last time they see him.

A WEEK LATER

A week passes. Max has not heard from any of the men and doubts that he will. Samantha has been unable to get in contact with Shepherd despite her repeated efforts. When she visits the university, she is told that Shepherd accepted a last minute offer to work on a project sponsored by a private party and abruptly left for South America. In spite of her resources, Samantha is unable to find any information about the project or the sponsor. A visit to Shepherd's home finds the house vacant.

Samantha follows up on some of the other participants. She traces the registrations on Corvus and Mr. Gideon's cars. Samantha's follow up investigation reveals that Corvus and Mr. Gideon have disappeared and no one seems to know anything about them, or are willing to talk about it. Carbonetti has been reassigned, but Samantha can get no additional information. Samantha's project is terminated and the Colonel is also reassigned. Information on his assignment has been restricted as top secret. She is ordered to stand down and wait for new orders. Samantha believes that O'Ryan is behind all the changes, but, once again, cannot prove it. Is it possible that the Nomads have members within the military? Or, is all this just coincidence?

TWO WEEKS LATER

Two weeks have passed and it begins to feel like a bad dream or an elaborate hoax. But if it was some kind of hoax, what was the purpose, Max wonders? And, how could Samantha have been so deceived unless there were more people involved than even she was aware, but again for what purpose? The fact is that Samantha did her best, but could find no evidence of a hoax or conspiracy. Deep inside Max knows the answer, but maybe he can convince himself otherwise. After much thought, Samantha decides the best option is to resign her commission.

Then, Max's phone rings early one morning. The caller does not identify himself, but Max knows from the voice it is Raymend. He is calling to tell Max that he has spoken with Shepherd and that Shepherd told him the whole story. He admitted that he suspected as much. But, he is also calling to apologize to Max and Samantha, for involving them in something they were better off not knowing. "So, is all this for real," Max asks Raymend. "I promised to tell you the truth and I would be lying if I told you what you want to hear," is Raymend's reply. "Good luck to you both," he adds and then hangs up.

Later that night, Max and Samantha sit on a porch, arm in arm and stare out at an azure sky accented by the warm orange glow of a sunset. Their senses have been heightened to the world around them. The joyful voices of children playing can be heard in the background. There is the sound of the leaves rustling in the trees as a gentle breeze blows. Words now seem insignificant. As the sun dips below the horizon, stars begin to appear in the blue darkness. Max and Samantha gaze at the stars knowing we are not alone.

The earth will go on, but will humankind be included in its future, Max wonders? Will we survive long enough to evolve and make the transition from a parasitic species to a symbiotic partner in the Universe? Or, will someone make that decision for us? Max still wonders if the world should know, but who would believe such an impossible story? Even as ever more violent and unprecedented storms rake across the planet, and seismic activity fractures the earth, it can't be; therefore it isn't.

EPILOGUE

As time passes, the easier it becomes for Max to pretend none of this ever happened. But then again, all he has to do is check the daily news to reinforce the reality.

In January of 2016, NASA established the Planetary Defense Coordination Office (PDCO) to oversee its ongoing efforts to detect and track near-Earth objects (NEOs). The PDCO's mission is to manage all NASA-funded projects to identify and analyze any asteroids or comets that will pass near Earth's orbit around the Sun. According to a NASA, asteroid detection, tracking, and defense of our planet is something that NASA and its interagency partners consider crucial. The long-term goal for planetary defense is to develop a means to detect or redirect NEOs bound for a collision with Earth; a capability the Nomads allegedly already possess. Curiously, it has been widely acknowledged the PDCO is a particularly well-funded initiative. Now the question becomes, "Given the current economic climate in which NASA must scrounge for every dollar it can get, how much money would be allocated on such a project if the danger is statistically insignificant? Or, is there another potential threat?" Max wonders.

Coincidentally, on October 12, 2017, asteroid 2012 TC4 will pass by Earth in what scientists are referring to as a near miss, hopefully no closer than its near miss in October 2012. Asteroid 2012 TC4 was first discovered on October 4, 2012, by an observatory in Hawaii and less than a week later passed within 69,000 miles of Earth. According to the most recent estimates, the size of asteroid 2012 TC4 varies from 40 feet to 130 feet across. In comparison, the space rock that exploded above the city of Chelyabinsk in Russia in February 2013 was estimated to be around 65 feet across and left 1,500 people injured and caused damage to thousands of buildings. Scientists admit there is still some uncertainty regarding the size and the orbit of 2012 TC4 and more observations are required. When discovered in 2012 asteroid 2012 TC4 was a relative surprise and scientists agree its orbit appears to be somewhat eccentric. How did it get so close to Earth so quickly without being previously detected? Whether the asteroid strikes the earth or does not, we are left to wonder, did the Nomads or did they not, have a hand in this?

Scientists have also confirmed that they have found "solid evidence" for Planet X on the fringe of our solar system. This ninth planet is estimated to be as big as Neptune, but has an elliptical orbit that takes Planet X billions of miles beyond Neptune's path. This vast distance suggests it would take Planet X 10,000 to 20,000 years to orbit the Sun. Technically, Planet 9, as Caltech researchers call it, hasn't actually been spotted yet, but its existence has been inferred through mathematical equations and sophisticated computer modeling. Researchers anticipate Planet 9's existence will be visually confirmed within five years as it circles closer to the earth. Is this possibly the planet Nibiru of Sumerian legend?

EM weapons development continues and has taken center stage in the U.S. arsenal. Electromagnetic railguns and lasers are two technologies the military is developing as an alternative to gunpowder or explosive propellants. General Atomics Electromagnetic Systems announced that its Blitzer railgun hypersonic projectiles successfully passed tests at the U.S. Army Dugway Proving Ground in Utah in March of 2016. Railguns launch projectiles using electromagnetic energy. The muzzle velocity of a railgun can be more than twice that of conventional weapons. The scenario is that a ship would generate electricity from onboard power plants and store that energy in a pulsed power system. The railgun then receives an electric pulse that generates the electromagnetic force. The force propels the projectile between two conductive rails attaining speeds up to Mach six (approx. 4,600 mph); three times faster that an average bullet. By adjusting the electromagnetic pulse, the range can be varied. This means the railguns will be able to strike threats more than 100 nautical miles away in approximately six minutes. Railguns could be deployed against a range of threats for precision strikes against land, water surface or air targets. Their lack of dependence on gunpowder and oxidizers, and velocity make them excellent weapons for deployment in space without violating any international treaties. This along with EM force fields to protect ships and EM-based body armor support the men's assertions of a new paradigm for future technology based on ET influence. Samantha knows that if the military is willing to publically reveal the existence of these technologies, the biggest secrets must be almost unimaginable.

Even more interesting, a team of scientists announced just recently that they had heard and recorded the sound of two black holes colliding a billion light-years from Earth. The sound of that collision was the first direct evidence of gravitational waves or ripples in the fabric of space-time that Einstein predicted a century ago. This discovery validates Einstein's vision of a Universe in which space and time are interwoven and dynamic in a universe that has the ability to stretch, shrink and jiggle. It also confirms the nature of black holes; bottomless gravitational chasms so powerful not even light can escape their grasp. The spawn of these gravitational waves is energy estimated to be 50 times greater than the output of all the stars in the Universe combined. Power we have been told the Nomads have harnessed.

Max has also noticed that over the last few years the U.S. and other governments have been uncharacteristically releasing formerly classified information about their UFO activities since the 1940s; activity, involving groups like the NSA, CIA, FBI and the military, that the public was previously assured never occurred. Again, why now, Max wonders? Is there a subtle message in these actions?

Scientists have also recently raised concerns that climate change may be affecting the rotation of the earth and causing it to wobble on its axis. It was suggested that the loss of mass from Greenland and Antarctica's rapidly melting ice sheet are one cause of this wobble. JPL scientists explored this scenario using observations from the NASA/German Aerospace Center Gravity Recovery and Climate Experiment (GRACE) satellites, which provide a monthly record of changes in mass around Earth. Changes in mass are routinely caused by movements of water through everyday processes such as accumulating snowpack and groundwater depletion. However, the scientist's calculations showed that while the changes in Greenland exacerbate the situation; alone do not generate the energy needed to cause such a noteworthy wobble in earth's spin. The scientists believe the answer is a deficit of water in the Indian subcontinent and the Caspian Sea. The region has lost a significant amount of water mass due to depletion of aquifers and drought. Although this loss is nowhere near as significant as the change in the ice sheets, the Earth's spin axis is very sensitive to changes occurring around 45 degrees latitude, both north and south, and why climate changes in the Indian subcontinent are critical.

Max Park has shared his experience with a very small circle of trusted friends who share his hope for the future. He wonders who else might know this story and how it has affected them. He parks his car in a crowded lot outside a Chinese buffet on a stormy, hot day and heads inside with Samantha to meet some friends for lunch. He pauses for a moment and looks up at the sky and wonders, has destiny has been taken by the hand?

ABOUT THE AUTHOR

RJ TELES, M.ED.

has been an investigator and "student" of the UFO phenomenon for almost 50 years and has worked with numerous UFO groups including NICAP, MUFON, NUFORC, and the Center for UFO Studies. During that time he has completed over 300 investigations and numerous interviews with military and government witnesses.

He holds a Master's degree in Information Technology Research and Development and worked as a technical consultant on cyber systems security, threat assessment and mitigation, and forensic data analysis for the government and private corporations. It was his work in these areas that gave him access to the military and intelligence communities where he met individuals willing to share their experience in regards to the UFO phenomenon and extraterrestrial life.